The junior church programme with a difference!

Three + One
A book of beginnings

Michael Forster

First published in 2000 by
KEVIN MAYHEW LTD
Buxhall
Stowmarket
Suffolk IP14 3BW

© 2000 Michael Forster

The right of Michael Forster to be identified as the author of this work
has been asserted by him in accordance with the Copyright, Designs
and Patents Act 1988.

The worksheets and dramas may be photocopied by the purchasing church
without copyright infringement, provided they are used for the purpose
for which they are intended. Reproduction of any of the contents of this
book for commercial purposes is subject to the usual copyright restrictions.

No other part of this publication may be reproduced, stored in a retrieval system,
or transmitted, in any form or by any means, electronic, mechanical, photocopying,
recording or otherwise, without the prior written permission of the publisher.

All rights reserved.

0 1 2 3 4 5 6 7 8 9

ISBN 1 84003 582 X
Catalogue No 1500367

Cover illustration by Jonathan Stroulger
Illustrated by Simon Smith
Edited by Helen Elliot
Typesetting by Elisabeth Bates
Printed in Great Britain

Contents

Foreword	5
Introduction	7
How to get the best from this book	9

Unit 1: Creation – in the beginning, God . . .

Overview of the unit	16
Week 1: Creation	17
Week 2: Fall	23
Week 3: Noah's flood	30
Week 4: All-age worship	36

Unit 2: Jesus – in the new beginning, God . . .

Overview of the unit	42
Week 1: New vision – the man born blind	43
Week 2: New priorities – the rich young ruler	49
Week 3: New attitudes – a woman in the synagogue	55
Week 4: All-age worship	61

Unit 3: Acts – in the Church's beginning, God . . .

Overview of the unit	66
Week 1: The gift of the Holy Spirit	67
Week 2: The conversion of Saul	73
Week 3: Peter and Cornelius	79
Week 4: All-age worship	85

Foreword

This series of books takes what might to many people seem to be a new approach to Junior Church teaching and all-age worship. In fact, though, it's a very old one – used, according to the Gospels, by Jesus himself.

First and foremost, Jesus valued people, cared about them, was concerned for their needs. He called people to become part of a community where they – many of them for the first time – were valued and enabled to feel that they were part of something worthwhile, that their lives had meaning and purpose. In the course of that, they learned a great deal and their commitment to Jesus and what he stood for grew until in many cases it was a life-commitment in more ways than one.

So the approach we take here is to focus on building relationships – including the children in something they may come to value, telling the faith story in engaging ways and letting the 'learning' be a spin-off benefit. I am convinced that that is a more effective way of working with children than focusing just on the imparting of knowledge.

People often complain that youth organisations do not seem 'interested in the Church'. The reality is that there is no *reason* for them to be interested: without faith commitment there is no other point in going to church when everything else it offers can be had more easily and more satisfyingly elsewhere. And that faith commitment will, I believe, be built more effectively, in their early years, by making them part of something they value *because it values them* rather than by trying to teach them things.

That brings me to the vital difference that sets this material apart. The sessions are arranged in sets of four: three 'Junior Church' sessions building into an all-age service on the fourth Sunday when the children's work will be celebrated and valued by the whole Church fellowship, and the adults will have the opportunity to learn both from and with the children.

I hope and pray that these resources will open minds of all ages to the wonder of God's love and the joy of sharing it, rather than merely fill them up with doctrines and ethical propositions.

All that will follow. The first thing – and the vital thing – is to *relate*.

Enjoy the book. Enjoy one another. Oh, and enjoy God, of course!

MICHAEL FORSTER

Introduction
(Please read this – I think you're going to like it!)

This series of books arose out of a particular need. We were finding the usual age-based 'classes' difficult to sustain in our context, and mixed-age groups seemed the only option – but the cry went up, 'You can't teach five- and ten-year-olds in the same class' (I'll have more to say about the 'teaching' idea later).

At the same time, we wanted to include the children much more in the actual planning of our monthly all-age worship which, until then, tended to be a bit of a one-man show that was done *for* rather than *with* them. But just when do you gather increasingly busy and pressurised children together to plan services?

This is what we decided to do. We would take an overall theme that could be presented in three weekly stories, and the learning process would consist of fun activities: story-telling, art and craft, drama, music, some of which could then become the basis for the all-age service. But what if some children could only come for two of the weeks? Would they be left out? Clearly, each week's story, while relating to the three-week theme, would need to be able to stand alone.

Wouldn't it make the all-age worship terribly long and overladen with material? Probably, if *all* the previous three-weeks' work were used – so the Junior Church would choose just one of the three stories as the focus for the service, but let the worship leader put it into context with the help of the pictures, models, etc., that the children had made. That would enable most of the art and craftwork to be on display in the church, providing a visual background to the storytelling. And storytelling really is the basis of communicating our faith. Ask any of our Jewish cousins! Or ask Jesus!

So this material was written, and some of it has been used, and the basic idea and format have been tried and tested. The result so far has been the releasing of some previously unrecognised creativity as children who had not been in the limelight before took the basic ideas and developed them in wonderfully imaginative ways. In the very first month of using this material, we discovered some real hidden treasure – and we did so in worship where we could properly celebrate and give thanks for it.

And that brings me to the most important thing we learned from this. Don't let the all-age worship become a talking shop! The discussion-type activities will quickly lose their appeal if that happens. We saw this coming in good time and proposed the setting up of a Worship and Mission Action Group (definitely *not* a committee) within the church to carry forward some of the ideas that come out of these sessions. Such a group must be a 'ginger group' rather than a management committee. They should not get bogged down in the minutiae of keeping new projects going, but simply research ideas and present possibilities to the relevant meetings (more than once if necessary!) to ensure that they are not simply lost in a sea of good intentions. If that were to happen – if the cards, etc., that the discussion groups produce were simply thrown away or filed and forgotten, we think it would not be long before the worship became stale: 'Oh, another of those silly discussions, again.' However, if the action group is set up, and enabled to work well, the all-age worship could become a real source of inspiration for the Church's mission – something through which the Holy Spirit might breathe renewal into the Church and the local community.

How to get the best from this book

The book is based on three 'units', each of which is a four-week cycle: three Junior Church sessions, and one all-age worship. Those Churches that currently have a monthly 'family service' will find it best to plan so that the 'fourth' Sunday in each unit falls on whatever Sunday of the month is appropriate for their system. (When there are five Sundays, that's not a problem – you'll appreciate the extra time to pull the threads together all the more firmly ready for the all-age service.)

Each session divides into a number of activities, and a worksheet is also provided either to do in the session or as a take-home resource. There will almost certainly be too much here for the single session of perhaps 45 minutes that most Junior Churches have – so *don't think you have to use it all.* (Nothing destroys a good learning environment like trying to cram too much in!) Choose what you think best fits your group in each particular case, and perhaps have other items standing by in case you run out. Much of course will depend on the number of children you have. A small Junior Church could work all together, concentrating on the story and just one or two activities, whereas a large one might start together for the storytelling and then break up into several multi-age groups, each focusing on a different activity – some children producing art and craft work, others doing drama, learning new songs, etc.

Similarly, you don't need necessarily to use all of sessions one to three. You may decide, in particular circumstances, to omit one session and spread the other two over the three weeks. The stories are written as stand-alone units, so you can do this quite easily. At the risk of labouring the point, the all-age worship in Week Four should be a celebration of whatever has been done – not a goal to be striven for and which becomes a blight on the sessions because the children are under pressure.

Most importantly of all, remember the central aims: the session should:

- be enjoyable for all concerned
- make all the children feel valued and cared about
- contribute to building relationships.

If you do these things, then the 'teaching' will happen, because children are great learners if the environment is right. They'll virtually teach themselves!

Let's have a look at each of the elements that comprise the sessions.

Thinking about it

This is vital – the advance preparation need not be unduly time-consuming or tedious, but it will transform the actual session. In fact, we found that the preparation required in using this material was much less onerous than preparing traditional lessons.

- A monthly meeting of key people would be a good idea, perhaps after Week Three, when you can pull together the all-age service and look ahead to the next four weeks.

- Decide which week's subtheme will form the basis of the all-age worship. You need to know this at the outset so that you will know which week's 'ticked' activity to prepare and which you can ignore.
- Then each week look through the relevant session thoroughly and give some thought to which would be the most appropriate and helpful elements to concentrate on, in your situation.
- Prepare any resources: art/craft materials, visual aids, legitimate photocopies, etc., that you need. Try to anticipate the kinds of questions the children might ask – or that you could helpfully ask them.

What's the point?

It's helpful to have a specific point in mind that we wish to convey. This does not mean we can't find other things in the text, but one point retained is better than five confused or forgotten – and more likely to engage the children's attention, too! They have the rest of their lives to explore the countless layers of meaning, so don't let's spoil it by cramming them too full of rich food!

Now for the session itself.

Doing it

Prayer

An opening prayer is offered. However, we should be careful about stereotyping prayer too much as merely 'talking to God'. It might be worth thinking about encouraging children to think of prayer as consciously *being with* God – sometimes quietly, but also in the more active parts of life. So let God join in the activities, the fun, most of all in the growing *relationships* between staff, parents and children. In a different kind of way, the whole session is 'prayer' – and both kinds are important.

For this reason, the prayers are short and are all focused in such a way as to point the children to that greater reality: the unconditional love of God.

From the known to the unknown

Jesus understood well the first principle of teaching: begin with what people know, and only then introduce the new. His most effective teaching, according to the Gospel records, was in parables. Often, he simply didn't mention scripture at all.

That is not an argument against biblical teaching – rather it is a plea to make it more effective. Children are wonderful at making connections – much better than we adults with our 'disciplined' (trammeled?) minds. So we begin by appealing to what they know, and *then* tell them the biblical story. With little or no prompting, they often will then grasp joyfully and spontaneously for themselves what we so often labour painfully and ineffectually to drill into them – and no one's more guilty of that than I am!

Tell the story

Story-telling is the basis of keeping the faith alive. Our Jewish forebears kept their children in the faith by telling and retelling vibrant stories, often around meal-tables, camp fires or in other informal settings, with plenty of song and laughter to help it along. So a child-friendly version of a Bible story is the mainstay of each week's material. It's a good idea to read it a few times in advance, so you are familiar and can half-tell, half-read it to the children with plenty of eye contact and other interaction. Or you can get them to tell it to each other by acting it out – see 'Drama', below. You may also find it useful to have some visual aids handy, or think of some questions you can ask, breaking off from the narrative whenever you choose to ask, 'How do you think God felt about that?' 'What d'you think happened then?' 'What would you have done about that?' etc. This will all help to maintain the children's interest – with a little imagination you can easily keep them enthralled!

Respond to the story

The children's response to the story now forms the basis of the rest of the session. It's important that they're encouraged to be spontaneous and really engage with the characters and the action. Here you will of course want to focus on the forms of response that are best suited to your situation, but the first one, 'Discussion', should never be missed out.

Discussion

Keep it lively, informal, chatty – and don't let any child feel silly or wrong, whatever they say or ask. The important thing is that they grow by being able to interact freely with the text. You may want to feed in some of their questions or reactions to the storytelling in the all-age worship. Most importantly, don't be anxious about this section – and don't let the discussion become either too long or too heavy! Just enjoy a bit of a chat with the children.

Song

Some songs are suggested. Either revisiting well-known ones or learning new ones can be fun, and perhaps sometimes the children can teach some of the new ones to the adults in the all-age worship. However, be careful not to let the Junior Church session degenerate into mere rehearsal. Let them have fun singing the songs, confident that even imperfectly sung they will still form acceptable worship. If some of the children have instruments, there's no reason why they couldn't be used at this time. All the songs recommended in these pages can be found in one or more of the following Kevin Mayhew publications (among others):

- *Kidsource*
- *The Source*
- *The Children's Hymn Book*
- *21st Century Folk Hymnal*

Art and craft

This will probably form quite a big part of the session: children of all ages and abilities can work together to produce models, drawings, paintings, etc. A few ideas are suggested, but they don't need to be limited. This was the area where we found children really showed their ingenuity and made immensely valuable contributions, producing and effecting ideas that would never have occurred to us!

Some of the art and craft work will feed into the all-age worship, and the items especially designed to do that are indicated with a tick. You may want to put less emphasis on this item if you're not planning on focusing on it in the service. What is important, in the 'ticked' activities, is that the children know *why* they are preparing these things – a few simple words of explanation will help them to relate it to the story they have heard and the point you were trying to make.

In terms of drawing and painting, the options are limited only by size of the group and the children's imaginations! They could build up over the three weeks a complete 'strip cartoon' of the whole story, to be used in introducing the theme in all-age worship. The pictures could be on a continuous frieze, or on cardboard placards held on poles by the children, or separate pictures fixed around the walls before the service starts. Children could enter at different points as the story is told, holding their placard, or – well, you think of your own ideas – they'll probably be better than mine, anyway.

Drama

The dramatised version of the story is included. It can simply be used as a dramatised reading, with different children literally reading the parts, or it could be developed if your group has a flair for it into something much bigger. Adapt it freely to suit your group. If you need more parts, try splitting the narrator's part between several children, or add in one or two new characters. During the free discussion of the story things might emerge that it would be good to include in the dialogue. Feel free to photocopy these pages and make your own alterations if you wish. The drama can then either be used simply as a teaching aid or rehearsed and presented in the all-age worship. An added touch might be to use a domestic tape recorder to record it – then each child could take home a recording of a play with their own voice on it!

Worksheet

This is included for you to use as you see fit. You could have some of the children colour in the pictures and display them at the service, or you could let a group work through the sheet as part of the session; or it could simply be given to them as a take-home sheet to help them remember the session and/or to share with their families.

All-age worship

This is the culmination of the unit, but please don't allow preparation for it to dominate and spoil the sessions. It's not a performance, and no one will mind if what the children produce isn't beautifully polished – the main thing is that they should be seen to be enjoying it.

The services are designed to be truly 'all age', involving the whole congregation, and – most importantly – giving opportunities for interaction across the age groups. There are no 'children's talks', but rather all-age activities. This approach needs to be reflected in the overall balance of the service, so that it is one in which all people can participate rather than a children's service with the adults as indulgent spectators.

Let's take a look at the various elements:

Songs

Naturally, there will be songs specifically chosen by the children, or at least with them in mind. But including some more 'adult' hymns not only shows respect to the older worshippers but also requires the children to sample a more varied diet and hopefully broaden their taste.

Welcome and statement of the theme

An example is given, but please feel free to use your own words and adapt it for your own circumstances. It's an important element in the service, for it introduces the chosen theme and sets it in the wider context. It is also a jolly good opportunity to point out some of the creative work the children have done, and have it suitably acknowledged by the congregation.

Prayers

Again, an opening prayer is offered, but it's not mandatory! Local worship leaders will probably want to do something more appropriate to the particular setting.

Word and action

The Bible story selected from one of the weeks 1-3 is not only read but reinforced with an all-age activity. The essential point is to make this at once meaningful and enjoyable. If people enjoy it, they're far more likely to enter into it. One important point, though: you know your own congregation best, and are in a position to ensure that people aren't treated insensitively. If you know that Mrs X doesn't like being in the limelight, then avoid drawing attention to her. Finally, watch the time. People will warm to the subject and be difficult to stop! You will also then be deluged with responses, many of them duplicated in different groups. Keep the discussion short and to the point, and move on. And don't forget to consider setting up the action group (see Introduction, page 7) – people need to know this isn't just a talking shop!

Offertory prayer

All we do and give is a free response to what God does for and gives to us. The offertory prayer is a good opportunity to highlight that point. This helps to avoid religion becoming 'works centred' rather than being a free, joyful response to God's grace.

Reading

Because you're using imaginatively rewritten stories, it's very important to read from a standard Bible in the service, and this point should never be overlooked. Children – and especially the older ones and the young people – need to hear the Bible read and come to appreciate it for themselves.

Talk

It's marked 'optional', but it's actually quite an important part of the service. As with the Bible, the traditional sermon is too valuable (when done well) to throw away. In a service of this nature, a short talk helps develop and maintain the skills of listening and reasoning. Keep it short, though, or it will have the opposite effect! On the other hand, if the service is running over time, this is an element that could *occasionally* be omitted.

Notices and family news

All too often, notices are regarded as an intrusion, and ways are often found to 'get them out of the way'. But surely, this is the life of the Church that is being shared here – and should it not be offered to God, along with the lives of his people? In the service order, I've suggested putting the notices directly before the Intercessions, so they can then feed into the prayers, thus integrating them more closely into the worship.

This is also a suitable time to do something else – the 'Family News'. People who have, for example, a birthday, or a wedding anniversary, or perhaps who are changing jobs, retiring or whatever, can share that with the congregation. A supply of cards can be kept in the church, with a suitably general message in them, to be handed out to people along with the good wishes and applause of the congregation. This is one slot we daren't leave out at Anstey, or we hear about it!

Intercessions

If Jesus was 'the man for others', it's hard to imagine worship that is genuinely Christian and doesn't include some sort of intercession for others. You will certainly want to include some of the children's own concerns that have emerged in the sessions in these prayers. You might also want to use some of the artwork to help the congregation focus on particular things. Whoever leads these, try to ensure that they are done thoughtfully, with a concern for the whole of God's creation, and not just Christians.

Closing prayer/benediction

Another element that should be kept short but meaningful! This is where the congregation are sent out into the world to live in some way the values and ideals they have expressed in their worship.

Now, go to it!

Most importantly of all – use the material imaginatively; make it work *for you*. It is your servant, not your director. What matters is that all involved enjoy the sessions, learn about valuing and being valued, build relationships with each other and with 'staff', and learn along the way.

That's how Jesus worked whenever he could. And it's not a bad example to follow!

Unit 1
Creation – in the beginning, God . . .

Overview of the unit

Theme: God the Creator and Re-creator

We take three key events:

Week 1: Creation

Genesis 1 shows God not manipulating creation but making space, creating opportunity, and calling life into being. It offers a wonderful insight into God's creative relationships, and how our own might reflect that – 'in his image'.

Week 2: Fall

The freedom God gives to creation makes the fall almost inevitable – and the resulting brokenness is beyond our scope to put right. Our only hope lies in the faithfulness of God. It was his gracious gift of freedom that was abused, and his response to that is not to abandon but to come seeking and calling his fallen creation. Could this be a new beginning?

Week 3: Noah's flood – a new beginning for creation

A completely new beginning – and yet it arises out of the old. God preserves a 'remnant', showing that nothing he does is ever wasted. That is the basis of real hope.

All-age worship

Here, you may choose to focus on any one of the three subthemes, but place it in the context of the overall story and theme: God's creative and redemptive grace. So while the specific theme chosen will be emphasised in the choice of 'Word and action' material, some of the art and craft work the children have done in the other weeks will be used to decorate the church and set the context of the wider story.

Important note

✔ The ticked activities in Weeks 1-3 are intended as the link material for the 'Word and action' slot in the all-age worship. You will only need to do this in one of the three weeks – depending on which week's subtheme is going to be the main emphasis in the service.

Week 1: Creation

Thinking about it

What's the point?

God's wonderful, loving creativity. In this story he gives creation space to grow; he works by invitation and response. What a wonderful model for our creative relationships with one another!

Doing it

Prayer

Thank you, loving God,
for this space you give us –
time and a place to be together,
to learn and to grow.
Help us to use it well,
and to come to love you more. Amen.

From the known to the unknown

Start with the area deliberately untidy and disorganised (but not *too* much so – you don't want to spend the whole session on this bit!). Get the children to help you make space to work. Separate out the pens from the paper, the crayons from the scissors, etc. Then point out that what you have just done is make space where something creative can happen. God works like that, too. Here's a story about God tidying up and getting creative!

Tell the story: Genesis 1:1-2:3

(See page 20 for a dramatised version of this story.)

Let's Get Creative

In the beginning, God decided to create the universe. To be honest, it wasn't very pretty at first – in fact, it was pretty untidy. And it was dark – really, really dark.

So God started by dealing with that. 'Let there be light!' he said. And there was. And it was good. And God liked it. So God separated it from the darkness. 'I'll call the light "day" and the darkness "night",' he thought. So of course the first day had gone.

Now, light's a wonderful thing – but as you know, it shows up an untidy bedroom something terrible. 'Man, what a mess!' said God. 'Better tidy up and make a bit of space to work. I'll make a start with all this water. Water's nice in its place – but this isn't in the place at all. What we need is a big dome – I can keep some of the water above it and some underneath, and that'll make a nice bit of sky.' And it happened, just as he said. And that took care of the second day.

'Now, let's see,' God mused. 'Let's have all the water under the dome pulled together so that some land can appear. That's terrific. So I'll call the land "earth" and the water "sea". Wonderful!'

And it was. With things tidied up a bit God had some nice spaces he could work in. So he spoke to the earth. Yes, I know it sounds silly, but if you're God, you can do that sort of thing – and it works. 'Let's see what you can produce,' he said. 'Lots of plants with seeds in them – and some trees, as well – lovely fruit trees with seeds in the fruit so they'll produce even more.'

In a flash, the dull brown earth sprouted millions of colours: lots of green stuff – can you think of any . . .? And trees with red berries . . .? And some yellow flowers . . .? And some fruit trees . . .? Well, all ways round it looked pretty amazing. 'That's great!' said God, but by then it was evening, and then came the morning: the third day had passed.

'Well, well, well,' said God. 'Morning already! Time to be at it. Let's put some nice lights in the sky – a bright sun for the day, and a gentle night-light as well – a moon's what we need, I think, and some pretty stars. Now, they could be really useful – they could help keep track of the seasons so we don't get rhododendrons blooming in the winter and catching cold. There, now, although I say it myself it's shaping up really well!' So the evening came, and then the morning – the fourth day.

'Right,' said God. 'Time to have a chat with the sea, now. Come on, you oceans – I want creatures this time. Lots of fish, great sea monsters, tiny little crabs – you name it, I want it.' [*So how about naming a few?*] 'Oh,' he went on, 'and let's have some birds flying in the sky, too . . . Oh, yes! Most satisfactory. Well, would you believe it – another day gone! What's that – I make it five.'

'Hello, hello, hello,' said God. 'Morning already? Well, time to talk to the earth again – it worked a treat last time. Now, you can produce lots of animals: everything from cows to creepy crawlies. Wonderful! Hey, I just *love* those horses in pyjamas! Right – what next? Well, what else could there be? Time for the real work of art. No, thank you, earth – I'm taking complete charge of this myself. This is special. I'll make people. They'll be like me, so they can think and love and be really creative – and they'll help the earth and all the animals and other creatures to do well – I'll put them in charge of it all and we'll work together. Yes, that sounds terrific.'

So God created people. He made them just like himself. He made both men and women, and he blessed them. 'Everything's ready,' he said. 'I've prepared a wonderful world for you. So go and have lots of children, and spread out over the whole earth to look after it. Care for the animals, as well, and for the fish and the birds – oh, and don't forget the flowers and trees. It's all your responsibility, now. There's lots of food for you and for the animals – oh, my Word, I'm happy!'

Did God say 'happy'? Ecstatic more like it. But time flies when you're enjoying yourself: evening came, and then morning, and the sixth day had gone.

'Just one more thing,' God said. 'I've got to invent rest – a day set aside for love, friendship, worship – anything but work. Work six, rest one; work six, rest one; work six . . . that's it – get some rhythm going. Now that's *really* good.'

Respond to the story

Discussion

What does this story tell us about how God loves us?

- That he wants to love us, not just control us?
- That he wants us to play a part in things?
- That he really values the things we do?

What can we learn about how we treat the world?

- That we are called to love it, and help it grow, not just get what we can out of it?
- That God intended it to be beautiful, not ugly?

Song

One or more of the following songs might be used here and/or in the all-age worship:
Let love be real*
Let us sing your glory, Lord
O Lord my God
Our God is so great
Send forth your Spirit, Lord
There are hundreds of sparrows

Art and craft

✔ Create a barren landscape, either by using a box of sand or by securing some pieces of oasis together. (See 'Word and action' in the all-age worship for how this would be used.) If you use sand, it will need to be firmly packed to allow things stuck into it to stand upright. Test it with a drinking straw. Now let the children draw rough outlines (no detail – the cards need to be blank for writing on) of flower heads and tree foliage on brightly coloured card. (It doesn't matter that the trees are the same size as the flowers – they can be very young saplings!) Make them about 10-12 cm across, to allow space for a few words to be written on them. Use sticky tape to fix the heads to drinking-straw 'stalks', and set aside for the all-age service. As an added feature, you might like to prepare a sign to go above the landscape with the name of your town/village/district on it.

Draw or paint a picture of the creation story as the children perceive it. It could be the dawning of light in dark space, or a beautiful landscape, or a 'big bang' type explosion – or whatever else the children think of.

This is the key picture, but you might want to do others in addition to it, such as some of the different stages in creation: land emerging from the water, brightly coloured plants, etc., animals, sun, moon and stars . . .

Drama

See the next page for a dramatised version of the story.

---

* The modified text in *21st Century Hymnal* is more appropriate than that in the *Children's Hymn Book* which originated as a love-song in a musical.

Drama: Let's Get Creative

As there is only one 'character' in this story, it's recommended that the narrator's part be divided between a number of children. You needn't limit it to three.

Narrator 1 In the beginning, God created the universe. At first, it was pretty untidy. And it was dark – really dark. So God spoke.

God Let there be light!

Narrator 2 And there was.

Narrator 3 And it was good.

Narrator 1 And God liked it. So he separated it from the darkness.

God I'll call the light 'day' and the darkness 'night'.

Narrator 2 So of course the first day had gone.

Narrator 3 Now, light's a wonderful thing – but as you know, it shows up an untidy bedroom something terrible – and God noticed.

God Man, what a mess! Better tidy up and make a bit of space to work. I'll start with all this water. We need a big dome for a sky – I can keep some of the water above it and some underneath.

Narrator 1 And it happened, just as he said. And that was the second day.

God Now, let's see . . . Let's bring all the water under the dome together so that some land can appear. That's terrific. So I'll call the land 'earth' and the water 'sea'. Wonderful!

Narrator 2 So having made a tidy space to work, God spoke to the earth.

Narrator 1 What?

Narrator 2 I know, but if you're God, you can do that sort of thing.

God Let's see what you can produce. Lots of plants with seeds in them – and some lovely fruit trees with seeds in the fruit.

Narrator 3 In a flash, the dull brown earth sprouted millions of colours.*

Well, all ways round it looked pretty amazing. God loved it!

Narrator 2 But by then it was evening, and then came the morning.

Narrator 3 The third day had passed.

God Let's put some nice lights in the sky – a bright sun for the day, and a gentle night-light – a moon, and some pretty stars. Now, they could be really useful – they could help keep track of the seasons so we don't get rhododendrons blooming in the winter and catching cold. There now, it's shaping up really well!

Narrator 1 So the evening came, and then the morning – the fourth day.

---

* Here you could add some of the ideas the children thought of.

God   Right – come on, you oceans – give me some creatures. Lots of fish, great sea monsters . . .*

Oh, and let's have some birds in the sky, too . . . Marvellous!

Narrator 2   Night came, and then morning. That was the fifth day.

God   Now, earth – you can produce lots of animals. Wonderful! Hey, I just *love* those horses in pyjamas! Right – time for the real work of art – and I'm taking charge of this myself. I'll make people. They'll be like me, so they can think and love and be creative – and they'll help creation to do well – I'll put them in charge of it all and we'll work together. Yes, that sounds terrific.

Narrator 3   So God created people. He made them just like himself. He made both men and women, and he blessed them.

God   Everything's ready – I've prepared a wonderful earth for you. So go and have lots of children, and spread out over the whole earth to look after it. It's all your responsibility, now. There's lots of food for you and for the animals –oh, my Word, I'm happy!

Narrator 1   Did God say 'happy'? Ecstatic more like it. But time flies when you're enjoying yourself.

Narrator 2   Evening came, and then morning, and the sixth day had gone.

God   Day seven. One thing left to make: rest – a day set aside for love, friendship, worship – anything but work. Work six, rest one; work six, rest one; work six . . . that's it – get some rhythm going. Now that's *really* good.

* Let the children suggest names here.

Creation looks a bit dull. Colour the flowers and animals to make it beautiful.

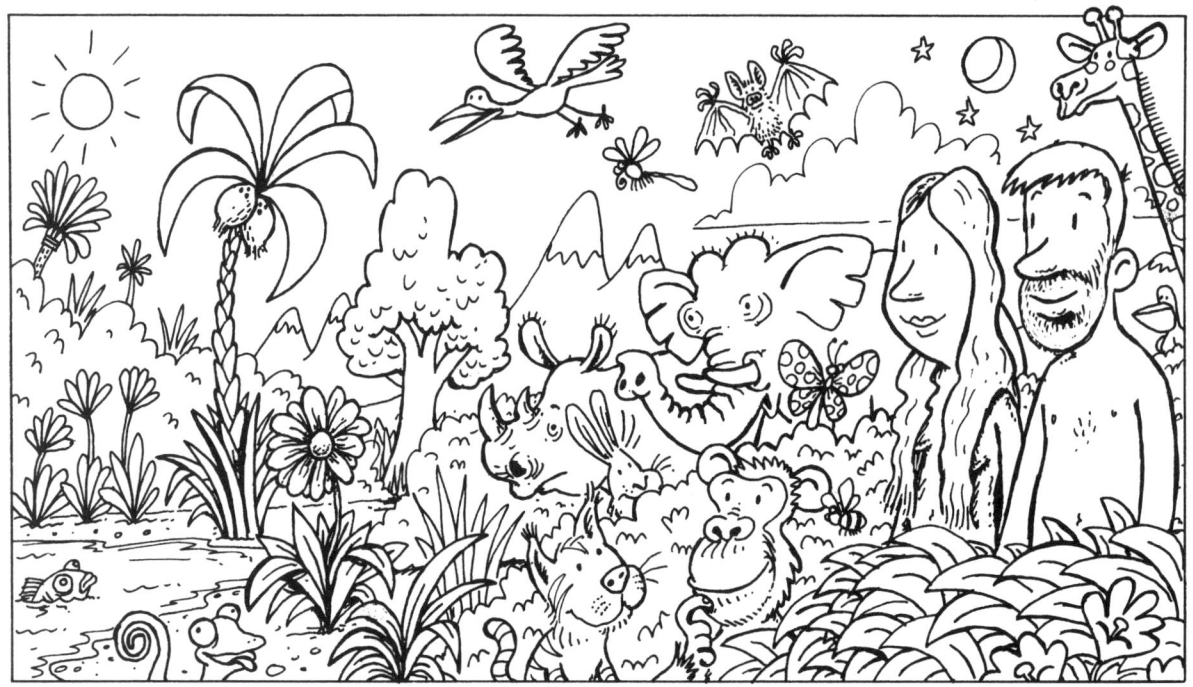

In the beginning, God created . . .

WORDSEARCH

Find the following words in the grid:

CREATION, UNIVERSE, LIGHT, DARK, SUN, MOON, STARS, EARTH, SKY, WATER, SEASONS WORK, REST, RHYTHM, NIGHT, DAY, MORNING, EVENING, BIRDS, ANIMALS, PEOPLE.

S	K	C	Y	M	O	R	N	I	N	G	B	
E	A	R	T	O	C	R	E	A	T	I	O	
P	C	E	S	O	S	L	A	M	I	N	A	
E	T	A	U	N	I	V	E	R	S	E	H	
O	S	T	N	I	M	S	E	A	S	A	S	
P	N	I	C	F	D	T	D	A	Y	R	K	
L	O	O	N	R	A	E	A	R	A	T	H	
E	S	N	I	W	O	R	K	T	G	H	Y	
U	A	B	N	I	G	H	S	K	R	A	D	
L	E	R	H	Y	T	H	M	O	S	K	Y	
T	S	E	R	O	G	N	I	N	E	V	E	
L	I	G	H	T	H	I	T	H	G	I	N	

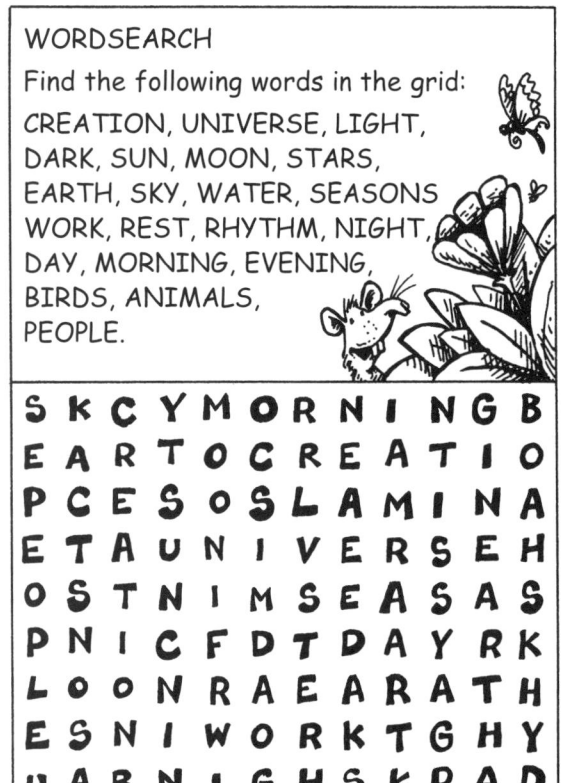

Colour the dotted shapes to find the creatures in the sea.

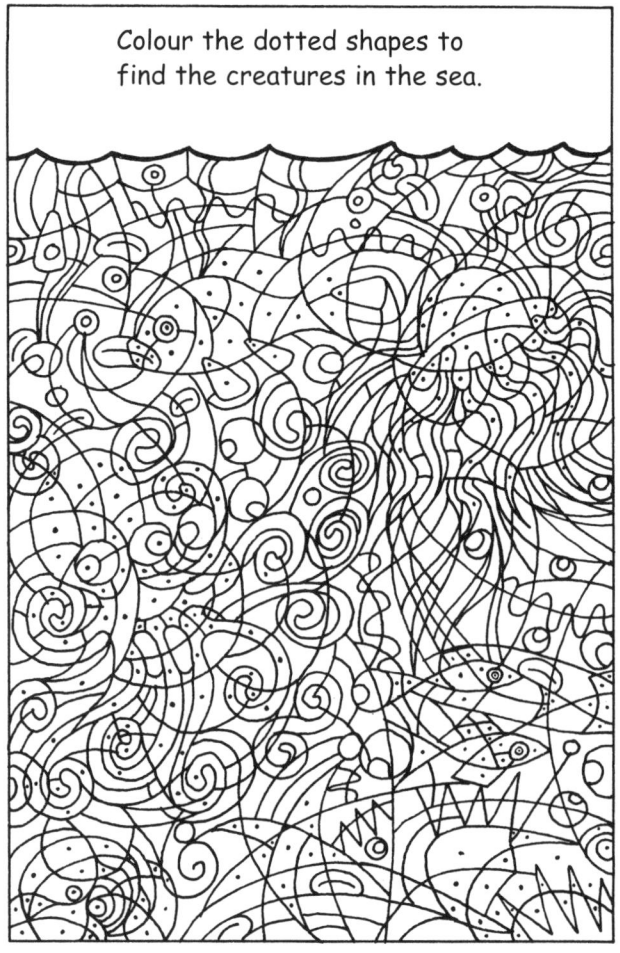

Week 2: Fall

Thinking about it

What's the point?

How the disobedient act of two people could somehow make us all sinful has occupied theologians for centuries. If we look carefully at the story, Genesis gives us a clue – it was not only the initial disobedience, but *the failure to take responsibility* (Genesis 3:12-13) which caused a catastrophic breach in the vital relationships in creation (Genesis 3:15) that has spiralled down the generations and affected every part of creation.

Children not yet ready for in-depth theological analysis can understand that point, and it's a very important insight for them to have. Present-day environmentalists show us how much easier it is to continue along that motorway to destruction, rather than take the rocky path toward the wholeness God intended for creation. However, God is faithful, and constantly comes seeking and calling 'Adam'. It's important today to make clear that God *has* provided for our redemption, but there's no need to go into detail.

Doing it

Prayer

Loving God,
we thank you for giving us each other –
for the friendships and the fun we enjoy.
Help us to learn to live together
in this wonderful world you have made for us,
and let all the things we share today
remind us of your goodness.
Amen.

From the known to the unknown

Have the children ever got the blame for something someone else did? How did they feel? Did it affect their feelings for the other person? Sometimes that kind of thing can permanently ruin a relationship – and often carry forward into succeeding generations. That's one reason why taking responsibility for what we do is so important.

Tell the story: Genesis 3

(See page 27 for a dramatised version of this story.)

We Did It Our Way

Adam and Eve had the most beautiful garden you could imagine, with all the different kinds of flowers and fruit: from daffodils to dahlias, from pears to pomegranates – you name it, it was there.* There were animals, too –

*So why not try to name a few?

all kinds of them, and of course lots of insects, and spiders. But Adam and Eve were never afraid, because the animals never attacked one another. They all lived happily together in the garden – that is, until the snake decided to stir up a bit of trouble.

'Hey, Eve,' it hissed one day, 'you know that tree in the middle of the garden, with the lovely fruit on it? Well, it's just that I've never seen you eat any of the fruit, and I was wondering why.'

'God's told us not to,' Eve answered. 'He's warned us that if we eat the fruit we'll die. That's the Tree of Knowing Good and Evil – and it's not good for us.'

'Oh, you silly human!' scoffed the snake. 'You won't die – you'll become like a god yourself. That's what God is afraid of! Go on – they're really tasty.'

The fruit certainly looked beautiful – round and shiny, and just bursting with juiciness and tastiness and sheer, gorgeous wonderfulness! 'Go on,' hissed the snake, soothingly. 'You know you want to.'

Well? Should she take the fruit, or should she do what God said and leave it alone?* Eve was tempted – *really* tempted. Slowly, she reached out her hand and just touched the fruit. How lovely and soft! She leaned forward and sniffed at it. Ooooooh! It couldn't really be bad for her – not when it felt and smelt so good?

'Go on – you know you want to. Why shouldn't you have the right to choose?' The snake's voice, along with the feel and smell of the fruit, was just too persuasive. Eve picked the fruit, and slowly bit into it. The juice squirted into her mouth and scored a bulls-eye on her taste buds. What a wonderful flavour!

Just then, Adam arrived. 'What are you eating?' he asked. 'Not the fruit from that tree, surely!'

'Oh, don't be such a fusspot,' said Eve. 'It's wonderful – here, have some.'

The smell of the open fruit was too much for Adam. He took it from Eve and bit into it. 'Oh, that's delicious!'

Suddenly, they heard a voice. 'Adam!'

'That's God calling,' gasped Adam, horrified. 'And we aren't dressed!' To be honest, they'd *never* been dressed – and somehow it hadn't mattered. But for some reason they couldn't quite work out, it seemed to matter now. Suddenly, they were rushing around the garden trying to make clothes out of leaves. The snake stopped hissing and started laughing – it had never had so much fun since the day it was created.

'Adam, where are you?' God obviously wasn't going anywhere, so Adam and Eve dived into some bushes to hide from him while they sewed their leaves together.

'I, er, I'll be there in a minute,' called Adam, '– just as soon as I'm decent.'

God sounded puzzled. 'What made you think having no clothes on was indecent?' he asked 'Have you been eating the fruit from that tree? *Have you disobeyed me?*'

---

* What do the children think?

'Oh, I'm not responsible for it,' said Adam. 'Eve tempted me – she's like that, you know.'

'Oh, start as you mean to go on, why don't you!' God answered. 'Blame the woman, as if you can't think for yourself!'

'Not my fault,' Eve protested. 'The snake tempted me.'

'Oh, so now we're blaming an inferior species, are we!' God exclaimed. 'And we'll have no hissing from *you* either,' he added to the snake. 'You've really let yourself down, you have – so down you can go. That's it – flat on the ground. And stay like that. It's such a shame – just as you were all getting on so well, too. Well, I'm afraid you've blown it. No more nice cuddles with the lions for you, or swimming with crocodiles. From now on, life's going to get painful, and you're going to be fighting and struggling for survival. That's not how I wanted it to be, but you disobeyed me, and there's no easy way back, now.'

Adam and Eve had to leave the garden, and just as God said, life got hard for them. They never got on as well with the other animals after that, and the world's never been quite the same since. But God never left them, or forgot about them and he *certainly* never stopped loving them. But that's another story. In fact, it's *lots* of other stories!

Respond to the story

Discussion

Why did Adam blame Eve?

- Because he didn't want God to be angry with him?

Why did he think it was OK to blame her?

- Because he thought she was there just to be used by him?

Can the children apply that to Eve's blaming of the snake?

What about our attitude to the wider creation today?

- Just there to be used by us?
- Our responsibility to love and care for it?

Song

One or more of the following songs might be used here and/or in the all-age worship:

God never gives up
The bell of creation
There are hundreds of sparrows
There's a seed in a flower
Think of a world without any flowers
We are one family together
When your Father made the world

Art and craft

✔ Let the children draw pictures of anything they like. (See 'Word and action' in the all-age worship for how these would be used.) The important thing is to use different colours of card for the backgrounds. Estimate the likely number of groups your congregation will divide into, and have a card of unique colour for each group. The drawings or paintings could be of anything, whether animals, trees, household objects, toys, etc. Then let them cut each picture into a number of pieces. The aim is to have enough for every worshipper to have a piece of a picture, and for the colour of card it's drawn on to help them match up with others when the time comes. Explain to the children that this is like the beautiful creation Adam and Eve broke – we're going to try and piece it back together again!

Draw or paint a picture of Adam, Eve and the snake in the garden. (Plenty of discreetly placed bushes would be a good idea!)

This is the key picture, but you might want to do others in addition to it, such as:

- The Tree of Knowing Good and Evil
- The snake slinking along the ground

Drama

See the next page for a dramatised version of the story.

Drama: We Did It Our Way

Narrator	Adam and Eve had the most beautiful garden you could imagine, with all different kinds of flowers and fruit – you name it, it was there. There were animals, too – all kinds of them, and of course lots of insects, and spiders. But Adam and Eve were never afraid, because they all lived happily together in the garden – that is, until the snake decided to stir up a bit of trouble.
Snake	Hey, Eve, you know that tree in the middle of the garden, with the lovely fruit on it? Well, it's just that I've never seen you eat any of the fruit, and I just wondered why.
Eve	God's told us not to. He's warned us that if we eat the fruit we'll die. *That's* the Tree of Knowing Good and Evil – and it's bad for us.
Snake	Silly human! You won't die – you'll become like a god yourself. That's what God's afraid of! Go on – they're really tasty.
Narrator	The fruit certainly looked beautiful – round and shiny, and just bursting with juiciness and tastiness and sheer, gorgeous wonderfulness!
Snake	Go on, you know you want to.
Narrator	Well? Should she take the fruit, or should she do what God said and leave it alone? Eve was tempted – *really* tempted. Slowly, she reached out her hand and just touched the fruit. How lovely and soft! She leaned forward and sniffed at it. Ooooooh! It couldn't really be bad for her – not when it felt and smelt so good?
Snake	Go on – you know you want to. Why shouldn't you have the right to choose?
Narrator	The snake's voice, along with the feel and smell of the fruit, was just too persuasive. Eve picked the fruit, and slowly bit into it. The juice squirted into her mouth and scored a bulls-eye on her taste buds. What a wonderful flavour! Just then, Adam arrived.
Adam	What are you eating? Not the fruit from that tree, surely!
Eve	Oh, don't be such a fusspot! It's wonderful – here, have some.
Narrator	The smell of the fruit was too much. Adam took it and bit into it.
Adam	Oh, that's delicious!
God	Adam!
Adam	That's God calling, and we aren't dressed!
Narrator	To be honest, they'd *never* been dressed – and for some reason it hadn't mattered. But it seemed to matter now. They rushed around the garden trying to make clothes from leaves. The snake stopped hissing and started laughing – it had never had so much fun since the day it was created.

God	Adam, where are you?
Narrator	Adam and Eve dived into some bushes to hide while they sewed their leaves together.
Adam	I, er, I'll be there in a minute – just as soon as I'm decent.
God	What made you think having no clothes on was indecent? Have you been eating the fruit from that tree? *Have you disobeyed me?*
Adam	I'm not responsible. Eve tempted me – she's like that, you know.
God	Oh, start as you mean to go on, why don't you! Blame the woman, as if you can't think for yourself!
Eve	Not my fault. The snake tempted me.
God	Oh, so now we're blaming an inferior species, are we! [*To snake*] And we'll have no hissing from *you* either. You've really let yourself down, you have – so down you can go. That's it – flat on the ground. And stay like that. [*To Adam and Eve*] It's such a shame – just as you were all getting on so well, too. Well, I'm afraid you've blown it. No more nice cuddles with the lions for you, or swimming with crocodiles. From now on, life's going to get painful, and you're going to be fighting and struggling for survival. That's not how I wanted it to be, but you disobeyed me, and there's no easy way back, now.
Narrator	Adam and Eve had to leave the garden and, just as God said, life got hard for them. They never got on as well with the other animals after that, and the world's never been quite the same since. But God never left them, or forgot about them – and he *certainly* never stopped loving them. But that's another story. In fact, it's *lots* of other stories!

UNIT 1: WEEK 2

Can you find the snake hiding in the picture?

The pictures look the same but can you spot 6 differences?

WORDSEARCH

Find the following words in the grid:
DISOBEYED GOD, TEMPTED, KNOWLEDGE, EVIL, GARDEN, SHAME, BROKEN, SNAKE, GOOD, ADAM, TREE, EVE, RESPONSIBLE.

```
D I S O B E Y E D G O D
O B E G D E L W O N K T
O A R G A R D E G E V E
K D G O R O O K L V E M
E A I L K E D B G I V P
T M B D G R S E S L N T
G H O R O N T S H A E E
O O D U O G R N A K D D
G I S P A K E A M O R E
S Y S N A K E K E R A V
S E D I S O B N E Y G I
R E S P O N S I B L E S
```

29

Week 3: Noah's flood

Thinking about it

What's the point?

A new beginning for creation. But God doesn't just throw away and start again. He uses a 'remnant' from the old to begin the new. There's a lot about this kind of thing in the Bible, and it's one way of showing that nothing God does is wasted – and he never wastes what's good in the things we do, either. That's why he's the God of hope!

Doing it

Prayer

Thank you, God,
for all the new starts you give us in our lives;
especially in our friendships and our families.
Be with us in all we do today,
and help us learn to trust you more and more.
Amen.

From the known to the unknown

Have you got a patchwork quilt, made from left-overs? If not, perhaps you can show the children an old, worn-out dress or a broken piece of furniture, and ask them what you might make of it. Could you save the buttons from the old dress to use elsewhere, or turn the top from a broken stool into a shelf? No doubt you and the children can think of many more examples of 'remnants' that can be used in new ways. God works that way, too. So he doesn't waste anything that's good.

Tell the story: Genesis 6:5-9:17

(See page 33 for a dramatised version of this story.)

Let's Begin Again

Now, why would a farmer want to keep lions? And why would he want to keep them on a boat? No, well, it wasn't Noah's idea of a good idea, either – and if it hadn't come from God he wouldn't have given it a second thought. But it did. So he had to.

'I'm not happy with things,' God said to him. 'The world's a terrible place, because of what people are doing – I'm going to start again. So build a boat.'

'Sorry, God, you've lost me,' said Noah. 'I don't somehow see the connection.'

'Water,' God told him. 'Lots of it – enough to flood the whole world and destroy everything so I can start again from the beginning.'

'You've convinced me,' said Noah. 'I'll build a boat.'

'Good man,' said God. 'I always knew you were – that's why I'm going to save you. Now you've got to take your wife and your family – yes, and the in-laws, too – and a complete selection of wildlife. You know, lions, tigers, cattle, that sort of thing.'

'I'll need a *big* boat,' Noah grunted – and got started.

The neighbours thought it was hilarious, and they used to gather in groups to watch Noah working and poke fun at him. Noah just ignored them and went on building. Then it was time to start rounding up the animals. 'Two of each,' said God. 'They've got to start off the new creation, so make sure they're good ones.'

Gradually, they got the zoo together.* The neighbours stopped laughing and started worrying.

'He's lowering the tone of the area,' said one.

'I can't sleep for the elephants' noise,' said another.

'It's not the noise, it's the smell!' commented someone else.

'Let's form a residents' association and get a petition against it,' someone suggested. 'This has always been a respectable neighbourhood.'

'Never mind them,' God said to Noah. 'You just stick with me, and do what I tell you. No, I know there's not a cloud in the sky yet, but there will be.'

Time went by, and one day Noah noticed the clouds beginning to gather. The sky got darker and darker, and a fresh wind began to blow. 'Hurry up, everybody,' Noah called. 'Get those animals on board!'

For a minute or two it was all a mad rush. The monkeys were on first, swinging up onto the roof by their tails, carrying bananas in their hands; the lions wanted a red carpet and their own private suite, because they were royalty – but Noah said that all animals were equal as far as he was concerned; and the giraffes complained that the cabin ceilings were too low. But Noah soon had them all sorted out, and they closed the hatches.

'Noah, haven't you forgotten something?' God asked.

'Er, I don't think so.'

God got stern. 'You don't go anywhere until the skunks are on board.'

'Oh, OK – but they're going as far away from my cabin as I can get them.'

Eventually, they were all accounted for, just as the rain started. The neighbours stopped laughing and ran inside to shelter, but the water just got higher and higher until even the mountaintops were covered.

'Phew!' said Noah, 'That was a close one. And talking of close, where have those fleas got to?'

For well over a month it rained and rained and rained. Then it took a long time for the water to go down, but gradually it did until the boat was resting on top of a mountain. God spoke to Noah again.

'Out you get, then – all of you. Let the animals go – we're starting off a whole new world.'

---

* Can the children suggest some animals Noah might have collected?

As the last of the animals ran off into the distance, Noah turned to his wife. 'I just hope we don't have to go through all that again,' he said. 'Why God made us take those cockroaches along beats me.'

'Don't worry, Noah,' God assured him. 'I'm not going to do this ever again – and here's a sign of my promise. Whenever you see a rainbow in the sky, remember that I've promised always to care for the world.'

Noah looked up and, sure enough, there was a brilliant rainbow in the sky. 'Come on,' he said to his wife. 'Let's make a new start.'

Respond to the story

Discussion

Why didn't God just start completely from scratch – why go to all the trouble to save Noah and the animals?

- Because God doesn't waste anything that's good?
- Because God values what's good about the 'old' as well as the 'new'?

Who was the main character in the story?

- Noah? (He was important, but he wasn't the power behind it)
- God? (Ah, that's better!)

Song

One or more of the following songs might be used here and/or in the all-age worship:

All of the creatures God had made
Rise and shine and give God the glory
The bell of creation
There's a rainbow in the sky
You shall go out with joy

Art and craft

✔ You're going to make a 'rainbow'. Get the children making paper chains from brightly coloured strips of paper – you can buy them ready-gummed from good stationers. (See 'Word and action' in the all-age worship for how this would be used.) The idea is to produce a number of lengths of chain that can later be joined together. The links should be in random colours, reflecting the 'rainbow' idea. Make sure you have enough extra strips for the congregation to use. As you work you can point out to the children that bright colours always help us to feel more hopeful – and we are people of hope because we believe in a God who saves and helps us.

Draw or paint a picture of a rainbow over the ark.

This is the key picture, but you might want to do others in addition to it, such as:

- the animals going into the ark
- the ark floating on the water during the flood
- any number of pictures of animals, or of Noah and his family

Drama: Let's Begin Again

Narrator	Now, why would a farmer want to keep lions? And why would he want to keep them on a boat? No, well, it wasn't Noah's idea of a good idea, either – and if it hadn't come from God he wouldn't have given it a second thought. But it did. So he had to.
God	I'm not happy with things, Noah. The world's a terrible place, because of what people are doing – I'm going to start again. So build a boat.
Noah	Sorry, God, you've lost me. I don't somehow see the connection.
God	Water. Lots of it – enough to flood the whole world and destroy everything so I can start again from the beginning.
Noah	You've convinced me. I'll build a boat.
God	Good man. I always knew you were – that's why I'm going to save you. Now you've got to take your wife and your family – yes, and the in-laws, too – and a complete selection of wildlife. You know, lions, tigers, cattle, that sort of thing.
Noah	I'll need a *big* boat – I'd better get started.
Narrator	The neighbours thought it was hilarious, and they used to gather in groups to watch Noah working and poke fun at him.*
	Noah just ignored them and went on building. Then it was time to start rounding up the animals.
God	You need two of each. They've got to start off the new creation, so make sure they're good ones.
Narrator	Gradually, they got the zoo together. The neighbours stopped laughing and started worrying.
Neighbour 1	He's lowering the tone of the area.
Neighbour 2	I can't sleep for the elephants' noise.
Neighbour 3	It's not the noise, it's the smell!
Neighbour 4	Let's form a residents' association and get a petition against it. This has always been a respectable neighbourhood.
God	Never mind them, Noah. You just do what I tell you. No, I know there's not a cloud in the sky yet, but there will be.
Narrator	Time went by, and eventually the clouds began to gather. The sky got darker and darker and a fresh wind began to blow.
Noah	Hurry up, everybody. Get those animals on board!

* What kind of thing might the neighbours have said? Why not add the children's own ideas for dialogue here?

Narrator	For a minute or two it was all a mad rush. The monkeys were on first, swinging up onto the roof by their tails, carrying bananas in their hands; the lions wanted a red carpet and their own private suite, because they were royalty – but Noah said that all animals were equal as far as he was concerned; and the giraffes complained that the ceilings were too low. But Noah soon had them all sorted out, and they closed the hatches.
God	Noah, haven't you forgotten something?
Noah	Er, I don't think so, God.
God	[*Sternly*] You don't go anywhere until the skunks are on board.
Noah	Oh, OK – but as far from my cabin as I can get them.
Narrator	Eventually, they were all accounted for, just as the rain started. The water got higher and higher until even the mountaintops were covered.
Noah	Phew! That was a close one. And talking of close, where have those fleas got to?
Narrator	For well over a month it rained and rained and rained. Then it took a long time for the water to go down, but gradually it did until the boat was resting on top of a mountain.
God	Out you get, then – all of you. Let the animals go – we're starting off a whole new world.
Noah	I just hope we don't have to go through all that again. Why we had to take those cockroaches along beats me.
God	Don't worry, Noah. I'm not going to do this ever again – and here's a sign of my promise. Whenever you see a rainbow in the sky, remember that I've promised always to care for the world.
Narrator	Noah looked up and, sure enough, there was a brilliant rainbow in the sky.
Noah	Come on, everyone. Let's make a new start.

UNIT 1: WEEK 3

I think that Noah's forgotten something. Quick! Draw a strong fence between the lions and the sheep.

Draw lines to show Noah which food to give each animal.

This is the sign of my promise. (Genesis 9:17)

```
T X A G A I T R A I N B
A P R O M I S E A T I N
O O C D O L F T S A V O
B E G I T S L A M I N A
R A I N B O P W A T E H
S A V E D C R E A T I A
A T I B E G I N N I N G
G E B N O I T A E R C A
A R L N B E G I N N I I
I W I M A O F L O O D N
B A O N E G W O R L K Z
R J N E W W O R L D G H
```

WORDSEARCH

Find the following words in the grid: GOD, PROMISE, NOAH, ANIMALS, BOAT, FLOOD, RAINBOW, RAIN, NEW WORLD, CREATION, SAVED, BEGINNING, AGAIN, WATER.

35

Week 4: All-age worship

Opening song

A song praising and celebrating the faithfulness of God

Welcome and statement of the theme

Get one or more of the children to point out or hold up the pictures as you sum up the story:

In Junior Church during the past few weeks, we've been learning about God as Creator. We read the story of his first creating the universe, creating order and encouraging creation to flourish; then we saw how sin broke the vital relationships between God and creation, but also between different parts of creation itself. But even then, God saved what he could and made a new start. Then we read the story of Noah and the great flood, where God saved enough of the old creation to start off the new.

That's the general picture, but today we're going to concentrate on: [*Name the episode of your choice*]

Prayer

– use whichever is appropriate

Based on Week 1

Great Creator God,
we thank you for all the beauty and wonder
of your creation.
Thank you for giving us
the privilege of working with you
to help creation grow and flourish.
Forgive us when we exploit for our own selfish gain
the wonderful thing you gave us to care for,
and help us to live and work
more closely with you.
Amen.

Based on Week 2

Loving God,
thank you for giving your creation freedom.
Thank you for taking our contribution to creation seriously,
even when we get things wrong.
Forgive us when we do that,
and especially when we blame each other
instead of recognising our own responsibility.
Help us to be more fully human
and to trust in your forgiveness and healing power.
Amen.

Based on Week 3

Loving God,
thank you for being a God of hope,
and always offering a new beginning when things go wrong.
Forgive us when we show so little faith in you,
and help us to trust you more.
Amen.

Word and action

– use whichever is appropriate

From Week 1

Have the story read in either narrative or dramatised form, and then draw attention to the barren landscape. If you've done the sign, you can say, 'Is this what our area's really like?' No doubt there are some aspects that are like that, but some that are not. Divide the congregation into groups and give out the card flowers. Ask them to discuss where the opportunities are for God's creativity to show in your area. Is there a thriving youth club that gives young people a healthy social outlet? Is there, perhaps, a Toc H or Round Table that provides a sign of God's goodness in the area, or a dramatic society that brings people of different ages and circumstances together? Are you particularly well blessed with your local medical or dental centre, or is there a nice park for people to enjoy? What about the gifts of people in or around the congregation? Do you have talented musicians, craftworkers, artists? Is the Church providing, or could it provide, important services to the community? What about the pastoral care that goes on in the Church? These are just examples of ideas that you might have in mind in order to prompt any groups that are struggling. Ask them to write the things they think of on the cards. If – or, rather, when – more than one group thinks of the same things, that doesn't matter. Having more flowers with that item on will show its enhanced value in the community.

After a suitable time, call the groups together and ask them to tell the rest of the congregation what they have written on their flowers, as they come forward and plant the flowers in the oasis or sand to make the barren landscape blossom with signs of God's creativity. Now *that's* what God calls us all to be part of – and it's a pretty exciting thing to be involved in, isn't it?

From Week 2

[Ask the door stewards to give each worshipper a random fragment of picture as they arrive.]

Have the story read, either in narrative or dramatised form, and then ask the door stewards to bring forward any remaining picture fragments to you so that they can be available to people as needed. Now explain to the congregation that they have to do something creative, in putting a broken picture back together again. To do this, they will need to interact with other worshippers, swapping cards according to colour until they can, between a number of them, assemble a particular picture. You could divide them into groups, and allocate a colour to each group, or simply let them sort themselves out. Either way, at least some of them are going to have to get out of their seats and move around. You will need a number of boards or household trays for them to use.

It doesn't matter if not all the pictures are completed – the point is that they had to relate to one another and co-operate in order to do it. No one person had the entire picture, and they may have had to co-operate with someone the other side of the building in order to make the picture whole again.

So, God is calling us to work not only with him but with other peoples and elements in creation, possibly far removed from us, whether geographically, culturally or socially, in order to make creation whole again.

From Week 3

Have the story read, either in narrative or dramatised form, and divide the congregation into groups. Give each group a number of the coloured paper slips, and tell them they are going to make a rainbow of hope. First, they will need to discuss how the Church can be a sign of hope to the people around. Could you, for example, think about a visiting/befriending scheme for lonely people? Is there scope for a regular drop-in for bereaved people? Are there local issues where the people would be encouraged if they saw the Church campaigning with them?

Ask the people to write the ideas they think of on their slips of paper.

After a suitable time, call them to order and produce the lengths of paper chain the children have made. It's a kind of rainbow – but it's all broken up. Ask representatives from each group to come forward and tell the rest of the congregation what they have written on their slips of paper. As always, it doesn't matter if more than one group has said the same things – it's probably significant that there is some greater support for those particular ideas. Use the slips they have brought forward to join up the sections of the chain and (according to its length and the size of your building) either drape it around some of the furniture at the front of the church or stretch it around the building. Just as God called the whole world to take part in the creation process at the very beginning, so he calls us to be a 'rainbow people' – to be a sign of hope, and to help him make rainbows in the communities where we are placed. You might like to invite people when they go home to break off a few links of the chain and take them home as a reminder of that calling. They might like to hang them in a frequently used part of the house, or to use them as a visual aid in their private devotions.

Song 2

Offering

This may be introduced as our offering of ourselves, our talents, our faith, for God to use in making creation whole.

Offertory prayer

> Loving God,
> we thank you for all the wonder of your creation,
> but most of all for the privilege
> of being partners with you in the creative process.
> Accept what we offer of ourselves and our possessions,
> that creation may once again be whole,
> and know the joy of perfect relationship with you.
> Amen.

Song 3

Reading

> Matthew 6:25-30 read from a standard Bible. Introduce it with words such as: Jesus reminds us of God's continued care for every part of his creation.

Talk (optional)

> If you feel it appropriate (and if time permits) point out that for all that's wrong with the world, goodness and beauty stubbornly refuse to be extinguished. One possible response when people say, 'How can you believe in a good God when the world's as it is?' might be to point out the very fact that goodness, despite its apparent frailty, survives against such apparently insuperable odds. So, what – or who – is keeping the flame alight in the storm?

Notices and family news

Prayers of intercession

> These could be led entirely by the minister or other adult(s), and/or could include some prayers written by the children themselves – or simply some points that they have raised in discussion.

Song 4

Closing prayer/benediction

Unit 2
Jesus – in the new beginning, God . . .

Overview of the unit

Theme: A new beginning in Christ

We take three key events:

Week 1: New vision – the man born blind

Is our vision so clouded by a legalistic view of religion that we can't see the good God is doing around us? It's an occupational hazard of all religious people. Some of us can even get legalistic about not being legalistic – if you see what I mean . . .

Week 2: New priorities – the rich young ruler

A man comes to Jesus, concerned with how he might assure himself of a place in heaven. Jesus surprises him by saying that being 'good' in an ethical sense isn't what it's mainly about. He calls him to engage with the needs of *this* world in a way that the man finds just too much. Indeed, it seems an impossible demand to many of us – but Jesus leaves us with the assurance that what may seem impossible to us is possible with God. We are reminded again that our hope is in God's grace, and not our good works. Gosh – what a relief!

Week 3: New attitudes – the woman bent double in the synagogue

Once again, Jesus confronts legalistic, works-centred religion in the name of all who are oppressed by it. The woman in this story is, in Jesus' words, not 'healed' but 'freed' and given a full place in God's purpose. So all who still today feel excluded from Church or society find their champion in Jesus.

All-age worship

Here, you may choose to focus on any one of the three subthemes, but place it in the context of the overall story and theme: Christ's new beginning. So while the specific theme chosen will be emphasised in the choice of 'Word and action' material, some of the art and craft work the children have done in the other weeks will be used to decorate the church and set the context of the wider story.

Important note

✔ The ticked activities in Weeks 1-3 are intended as the link material for the 'Word and action' slot in the all-age worship. You will only need to do this in one of the three weeks – depending on which week's subtheme is going to be the main emphasis in the service.

Week 1: New vision – the man born blind

Thinking about it

What's the point?

A new vision of God. There are none so blind as those who will not see! This man, although physically blind, could 'see' things other people couldn't – especially the spiritually blind Pharisees. Their idea of religion as a matter of keeping rules had hardened their hearts and blinded their insight, so when the God of love stood right before their eyes they couldn't recognise him. All too often our religion can get like that, too – but Jesus can give us a new vision of a God who loves us and longs for us to have *real* life!

Doing it

Prayer

Loving God,
thank you for showing us your love in one another.
Help us to see that this morning,
through the things we do together. Amen.

From the known to the unknown

Have the children ever been in a dark room and seen what looked like strange, frightening shapes that turned out, when the light was switched on, to be harmless piles of clothes or shadows on the wall? (Keep this light and humorous, and let the children know that we all have those experiences and there's nothing silly about it.) Sometimes, God can seem frightening because we're not seeing him clearly, but Jesus helps us to see more clearly – if we're willing to!

Tell the story: John 9:1-41

(See page 46 for a dramatised version of this story.

Can't See the Love for the Rules

Seth was having just another ordinary day – until Jesus walked by, and that changed his life for ever. The first he knew of it was when he heard one of Jesus' friends ask him a question – Seth couldn't see Jesus because he was blind, but his hearing was really sharp.

'OK then,' Seth heard one of them say, 'Whose sin made this man blind – was it something he did wrong, or something his parents did?'

Seth could have been very angry, but he was used to that kind of silliness by now. He didn't know who these people were, but perhaps if he ignored them they'd go and irritate someone else. Then he heard another voice, answering. And it made him pay attention.

'Oh, grow up!' said the voice. 'You can't blame either him or his parents for this – but as he's blind it's a chance to show God's love.'

Seth waited for the usual pat on the head and quick blessing he sometimes got. He found it really annoying – people thought they were being nice by treating him like a pet poodle, and he knew they meant well but wished they'd do something really helpful.

Suddenly, Seth felt something warm and sticky being put on his eyes. Jesus had made some mud from the sand on the ground.

Seth wasn't impressed. 'Hey, what's the idea!'

'Don't worry,' came the kind voice. 'Go and wash that off in the pool.'

'You bet I will – what a liberty!' Seth went off angrily to the pool they called Siloam. He quickly scooped up the water in his hands and washed his eyes. 'Eh? What's that?' Suddenly he could see a bright light. Then he began to make out shapes. He could see! For the first time ever! He started shouting for joy, and people began to notice. Well, they would, wouldn't they?

'Oh, so you can see, can you? So why were you begging for money before?' someone demanded.

'Well, I couldn't see, then,' Seth answered. 'It's a miracle.'

'Oh, very convenient,' sneered Simon, the Pharisee. 'When it suited you to be a beggar you were blind, and now for some reason you've decided to admit you can see.'

'It's not like that,' Seth protested. 'I *was* blind – but this man put something on my eyes, and now I can see.'

Simon pricked up his ears. 'I bet "someone" was that Jesus,' he thought. He turned to Seth. 'Well, whoever he was, he's a bad man,' he said. 'He was working on the official day of rest – and that's against God's law.'

Suddenly, the people around were arguing among themselves; no one could agree whether Jesus was a great man of God or a criminal! So Simon and the other Pharisees turned to Seth. 'Who do *you* think he is? After all, it was your eyes he opened!'

Seth couldn't believe his ears. 'He's a great prophet, of course,' he answered. 'It's obvious, isn't it?'

Simon and his friends weren't expecting that. Seth knew jolly well what they'd wanted him to say – that Jesus was a bad man – so they called Seth's parents. 'Your son hasn't really always been blind, has he?' they said. 'Own up, now – it was all a big con, wasn't it?'

'Oh, no,' said Seth's dad, 'he was blind alright – we're really thrilled about this.'

'Oh, you are, are you? So who do *you* think Jesus is?' Simon challenged him.

Seth's dad wasn't going to get caught like that. He knew that anyone who said good things about Jesus got banned from going to worship ever again. 'Seth's a big boy now,' he said. 'Ask him.' And he took his wife's arm and hurried quickly away.

Simon turned back to Seth. 'Come on,' he said, 'admit it – Jesus is a crook, isn't he?'

Seth looked patient. 'That's not for me to say,' he said. 'But I do know that once I was blind, and now I can see. And if it comes to that, I can see the blindingly obvious when it's right in front of me, which is more than you can, and you reckon you're not blind! It's all those precious rule books – you can't see past them!'

Simon was furious. 'Oh, you're a bad lot,' he shouted angrily. 'You always have been. You were born bad, and bad is what you'll always be. Never darken the door of my synagogue again.'

'Suits me,' Seth retorted. 'My eyes have been opened to see what's good. I don't want to end up blind to it again, like you. Now, where's this Jesus fellow got to – I think it's time we had a word.'

Respond to the story

Discussion

How do the children think it felt to be able to see after all that time?
- Ecstatic?
- Curious – wanting to know what the colours were called, and what things were?

Why were the Pharisees so frightened by this event?
- Because the man could 'see' through their hypocrisy, too?

What could the man see that they couldn't – even though they had their eyesight?
- That Jesus was good – or more than that?
- That they'd got their ideas about God all wrong?
- That they had turned a wonderful religion into a cruel one?

Song

One or more of the following songs might be used here and/or in the all-age worship:

Be still, for the presence of the Lord
Lord, the light of your love is shining
The Spirit lives to set us free (Walk in the light)
This little light of mine

Art and craft

✔ Draw a large picture of a donkey with no tail. Then cut it out and paste it onto another piece of paper or card. That should leave a definable ridge around the outline which is not obvious from a distance. (See 'Word and action' in the all-age worship for how this would be used.) Draw a tail on a separate piece of card, or make one from string and attach a drawing pin to the 'body' end. Make sure the children understand why they're doing this – they're going to help the congregation learn something about blindness!

Draw or paint a picture of Jesus with the blind man.

This is the key picture, but you might want to do others in addition to it, such as:

- the man washing his eyes in the pool
- the man arguing with the Pharisees
- some of the things the man could see when he opened his eyes for the first time

Drama: Can't See the Love for the Rules

Narrator	Seth was having just another ordinary day – until Jesus walked by, and that changed his life for ever. The first he knew of it was when he heard one of Jesus' friends ask him a question.
Disciple	OK then, whose sin made this man blind – was it something he did wrong, or something his parents did?
Narrator	Seth could have been very angry, but he was used to that kind of silliness by now. He didn't know who these people were, but perhaps if he ignored them they'd go and irritate someone else. Then he heard another voice, and it made him pay attention.
Jesus	Oh, grow up! You can't blame either him or his parents for this – but as he's blind it's a chance to show God's love.
Narrator	Seth waited for the usual pat on the head and quick blessing he sometimes got. He found it really annoying – people thought they were being nice by treating him like a pet poodle. But instead, he felt something warm and sticky being put on his eyes. Jesus had made some mud from the sand on the ground.
Seth	Hey, what's the idea!
Jesus	Don't worry. Go and wash that off in the pool.
Seth	[*Angrily*] You bet I will – what a liberty!
Narrator	Seth went off angrily to the pool they called Siloam. He quickly scooped up the water in his hands and washed his eyes.
Seth	Eh? What's that?
Narrator	He could see a bright light. Then he began to make out shapes. He could see! For the first time ever! He started shouting for joy, and people began to notice. Well, they would, wouldn't they?
Bystander	Oh, so you can see, can you? So why were you begging for money before?
Seth	Well, I *couldn't* see, then. It's a miracle.
Simon	Oh, very convenient! When it suited you, you were blind, and now for some reason you've decided to admit you can see.
Seth	Trust a Pharisee to say something like that! It's simple – I *was* blind, but someone put something on my eyes, and now I can see.
Simon	[*Aside*] I bet 'someone' was that Jesus. [*To Seth*] Well, whoever he was, he's a bad man. He was working on the official day of rest – and that's against God's law.
Narrator	Suddenly, the people around were arguing among themselves; no one could agree whether Jesus was a great man of God or a criminal! So Simon and the other Pharisees turned to Seth.

Simon	Who do *you* think he is? After all, it was your eyes he opened!
Seth	He's a great prophet, of course. It's obvious, isn't it?
Narrator	Simon and his friends weren't expecting that. Seth knew jolly well what they'd wanted him to say – that Jesus was a bad man – so they called Seth's parents.
Simon	Your son hasn't really always been blind, has he? Own up, now – it was all a big con, wasn't it?
Seth's dad	Oh, no, he was blind alright – we're really thrilled about this.
Simon	Oh, you are, are you? So who do *you* think Jesus is?
Seth's dad	[*Aside*] I'm not going to get caught like that. I know that anyone who says good things about Jesus gets banned from going to worship ever again. [*To Simon*] Seth's a big boy now. Ask him.
Narrator	And he took his wife's arm and hurried quickly away.
Simon	[*To Seth*] Come on, admit it – Jesus is a crook, isn't he?
Seth	That's not for me to say, but I do know that once I was blind, and now I can see. And if it comes to that, I can see the blindingly obvious when it's right in front of me, which is more than you can, and you reckon you're not blind! It's all those precious rules – you can't see past them!
Simon	[*Angrily*] Oh, you're a bad lot – you always have been. You were born bad, and bad is what you'll always be. Never darken the door of my synagogue again.
Seth	Suits me. My eyes have been opened to see what's good. I don't want to end up blind to it again, like you. Now, where's this Jesus fellow got to – I think it's time we had a word.

THREE + ONE: A BOOK OF BEGINNINGS

Jesus is helping the blind man to see.
Can you find 5 things that God gives us now to help us to see better?

WORDSEARCH

Find the following words in the grid:
BLINDNESS, SIGHT, HEALING, MIRACLE, SIN, SILOAM, WASHED, JESUS, PHARISEE, PREJUDICE, TRUTH, TRUST, REST, WORK.

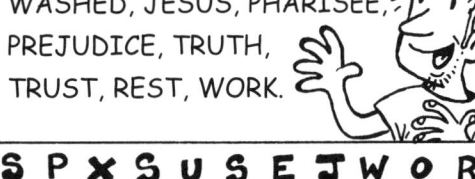

```
S P X S U S E J W O R K
I H E A L I N G S I L O
L A B L I N D N E F S R
P R E J U D I C E S E K
O I A T R U T R E L S T
A S L M S S E N C I L B
M E I A I E W A S H E D
T E N O R P R E J U D I
H R G L M I R A X L E C
G E U I M I R A C L O P
I J G S S E N D N I L B
S I L O T R U T H K I S
```

Crack the code to get a very important message.

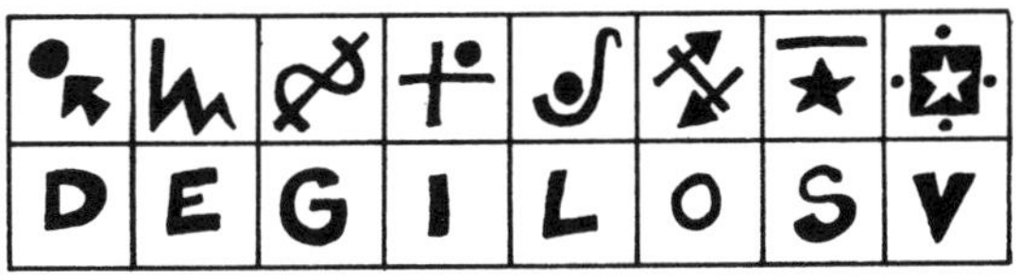

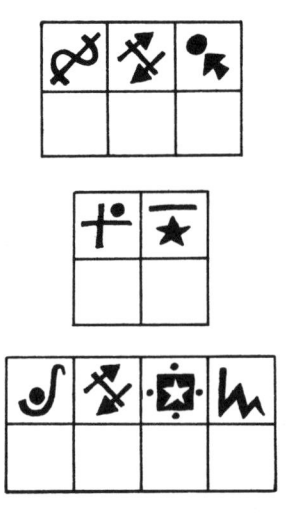

●	m	⚬	†	♪	⚡	★	✦
D	E	G	I	L	O	S	V

Week 2: New priorities – the rich young ruler

Thinking about it

What's the point?

Jesus calls us to a radical new outlook. While we may not feel called to take the drastic action suggested here, we do need to get things in proportion. We can't do without possessions, and everyone needs enough money to live reasonably, but the *real* treasure is the joy and the love we can experience by giving.

Doing it

Prayer

Lord Jesus,
as you love us so much,
help us to care for one another,
and for those who have so much less than we do.
Help us this morning to learn more about your love
and about the joy we can get from sharing it.
Amen.

From the known to the unknown

Ask the children about their ambitions, and then ask how they expect to attain them. Will they have to make choices? Will they have to be disciplined in the way they study, or the things they eat (whoever heard of an overweight jockey!). It may not mean giving up things they like altogether, but it will mean not letting the wrong things assume the greatest importance. That was the choice the young man in our story was faced with.

Tell the story: Luke 18:18-30

(See page 52 for a dramatised version of this story.)

Faith Is Too Expensive

Jonathan was really excited. He was going to go and see Jesus, and he'd get the chance to ask what he'd always wanted to know. Was he doing all the right things to be sure of going to heaven when he died?

He wanted to make a good impression – show Jesus he respected him. So he said, 'Excuse me, good and wise teacher, but can you tell me what I have to do to get to heaven?'

'Save the flattery for God,' Jesus told him. 'He's the only one you should be calling good. But anyway, you know God's laws – don't be unfaithful to your wife, don't murder, don't nick what isn't yours; don't tell lies about people; respect your mum and dad.'

'Oh, that!' Jonathan answered, proudly. 'I've kept all those rules ever since I was a nipper. Oh, yes – you wouldn't catch me doing terrible things to other people – and I always said 'please' and 'thank you' when I was asking my parents for more pocket money. Well, I wouldn't have got it if I didn't, would I? I didn't get where I am today by being naughty. That's why God's blessed me so much, you see – because I'm good. So, I'm OK then, am I? Jolly good! Bye!'

'Hang on a minute!' Jesus protested. 'I haven't quite finished yet – there is one thing you still need to do. You've got a lot of money, haven't you?'

Jonathan smiled modestly. 'Oh, I've done alright, I suppose.'

'Well then,' Jesus beamed at him, 'now's your chance to do even better.'

Jonathan was really excited – what was Jesus going to say to him?

'Sell everything you've got,' Jesus told him.

'What – *everything*?'

'Everything – the house, the stables, the racing camels, the sports chariot . . .'

Jonathan gasped. He couldn't be serious! 'Not – not the sports chariot!' he said. 'D'you have any idea what that special paint job cost?'

'The sports chariot,' Jesus insisted firmly. 'You won't need it any more. Sell the lot, and give the money to the poor people – now they really *do* need it. Then you'll have treasure stored up in heaven, and you can come and follow me.'

Jonathan stared hard at Jesus, looking for some sign that he was joking, perhaps a little twitching of the corners of his mouth? No? Well, a sparkle in his eye, then? No, not that, either. Jesus really was serious – he'd never been more serious since the day he told his mum he was leaving the family business. Oh, yes, Jesus knew how serious giving everything up was – and he'd never joked about a thing like that.

Jesus felt sorry for Jonathan as he stood there with his head down as though he'd never realised before how fascinating his shoes were. Jesus knew what was going through his mind – treasure in heaven sounded wonderful, but he couldn't see it or touch it. The treasure he'd saved up on earth seemed somehow more real. Much as he wanted to follow Jesus, it was too much to ask. Slowly, ever so slowly, Jonathan turned and walked gloomily away. Jesus looked at him kindly as he did so, before turning to his disciples and saying with a sad tone in his voice: 'How hard it is for people with lots of wealth to get involved in God's work! You know, I often think it would be easier for a camel to go through the eye of a needle than for a rich person to join our team.'

The people around gasped. Everyone knew a camel couldn't go through the eye of a needle. Why, it was hard enough even to get a bit of cotton through – let alone a ten-foot-tall camel, hump and all! 'Well, in that case, who *can* get into God's kingdom?' they started asking.

Jesus smiled. 'You're right – so it's a good thing you don't have to manage it alone, isn't it? I mean, it's pretty impossible for a human being, but with God anything's possible.'

Well – that's a relief! In that case, there's hope for us all!

Respond to the story

Discussion

Why do the children think the man was so sad when he walked away?

- Because he was too attached to his wealth?
- Because he really wanted to follow Jesus, but just couldn't face the cost?

Jesus probably lost a convert, here – should he have taken a different approach?

- Pretended it was easy, and let the man find out *after* he was committed?

Song

One or more of the following songs might be used here and/or in the all-age worship:
It's me, it's me, it's me, O Lord
Jesus had all kinds of friends
Lord, I want to be in your family
Take my hands, Lord
We are kingdom kids

Art and craft

✔ Make a treasure chest from an old shoebox or similar. Paint it gold and write on it '[Your Church's] Treasure'. (See 'Word and action' in the all-age worship for how this would be used.) Using teacups or coffee mugs as templates, draw some circles on yellow card and cut them out – enough for each of the groups in the congregation to have a few.

Draw or paint a picture of the rich man talking to Jesus.

This is the key picture, but you might want to do others in addition to it, such as:

- The man walking away, as Jesus watches
- Precious possessions – any expensive things the children think the man might have possessed: jewellery, gold and silver goblets, etc.

Drama

See the next page for a dramatised version of the story.

Drama: Faith Is Too Expensive

Narrator   Jonathan was really excited. He was going to go and see Jesus, and he'd get the chance to ask what he'd always wanted to know. Was he doing all the right things to be sure of going to heaven when he died? He wanted to make a good impression – show Jesus he respected him.

Jonathan   Excuse me, good and wise teacher, but can you tell me what I have to do to get to heaven?

Jesus   Save the flattery for God – he's the only one you should be calling good. But anyway, you know God's laws – don't be unfaithful to your wife, don't murder, don't nick what isn't yours; don't tell lies about people; respect your mum and dad.

Jonathan   [*Proudly*] Oh, that! I've kept all those rules ever since I was a nipper. Oh, yes – you wouldn't catch me doing terrible things to other people – and I always said 'please' and 'thank you' when I was asking my parents for more pocket money. Well, I wouldn't have got it if I didn't, would I? I didn't get where I am today by being naughty. That's why God's blessed me so much, you see – because I'm good. So, I'm OK then, am I? Jolly good! Bye!

Jesus   Hang on a minute! I haven't quite finished yet – there is one thing you still need to do. You've got a lot of money, haven't you?

Jonathan   [*Smiling modestly*] Oh, I've done alright, I suppose.

Jesus   Well then, now's your chance to do even better.

Narrator   Jonathan was really excited – what was Jesus going to say?

Jesus   Sell everything you've got.

Jonathan   What – *everything*?

Jesus   Everything – the house, the stables, the racing camels, the sports chariot . . .

Jonathan   [*Gasps*] You can't be serious! Not – not the sports chariot! D'you have any idea what that special paint job cost?

Jesus   [*Firmly*] The sports chariot. You won't need it any more. Sell the lot, and give the money to the poor people – now they really *do* need it. Then you'll have treasure stored up in heaven, and you can come and follow me.

Narrator   Jonathan and all the people watching stared hard at Jesus, looking for some sign that he was joking.

Jonathan   Can anyone see perhaps a little twitching of the corners of his mouth?

Bystander 1   No. Nothing's twitching.

Jonathan   Well, a sparkle in his eye, then?

Bystander 2   No, not that, either.

Bystander 3 You know, I think he really *is* serious.

Jesus I've never been more serious since the day I told my mum I was leaving the family business. Oh, yes, I know how serious giving everything up is – and I'd never joke about a thing like that.

Narrator Jesus felt sorry for Jonathan as he stood there with his head down as though he'd never realised before how fascinating his shoes were. Jesus knew what was going through his mind.

Jonathan [*Aside*] Treasure in heaven sounds great, but I can't see or touch it. The treasure I've saved up on earth seems somehow more – well, more real. I want to follow Jesus, but it's too much to ask.

Narrator Ever so slowly, Jonathan turned and walked gloomily away. Jesus looked at him kindly as he did so, before turning to his disciples.

Jesus [*Sadly*] How hard it is for people with lots of wealth to get involved in God's work! You know, I often think it would be easier for a camel to go through the eye of a needle than for a rich person to join our team.

Narrator The people around gasped.

Bystander 1 Everyone knows a camel can't go through the eye of a needle.

Bystander 2 It's hard enough even to get a bit of cotton through – let alone a ten-foot-tall camel, hump and all!

Bystander 3 So, who *can* get into God's kingdom?

Jesus You're right – so it's a good thing you don't have to manage it alone, isn't it? I mean, it's pretty impossible for a human being, but for God anything's possible.

Narrator Well – that's a relief! In that case, there's hope for us all!

THREE + ONE: A BOOK OF BEGINNINGS

Crack the code to find the title of a famous pop song.

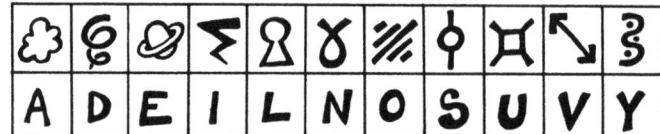

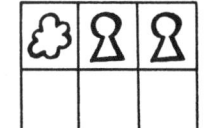

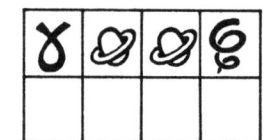

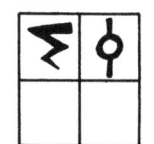

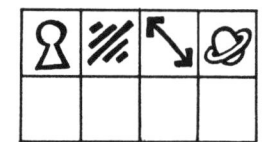

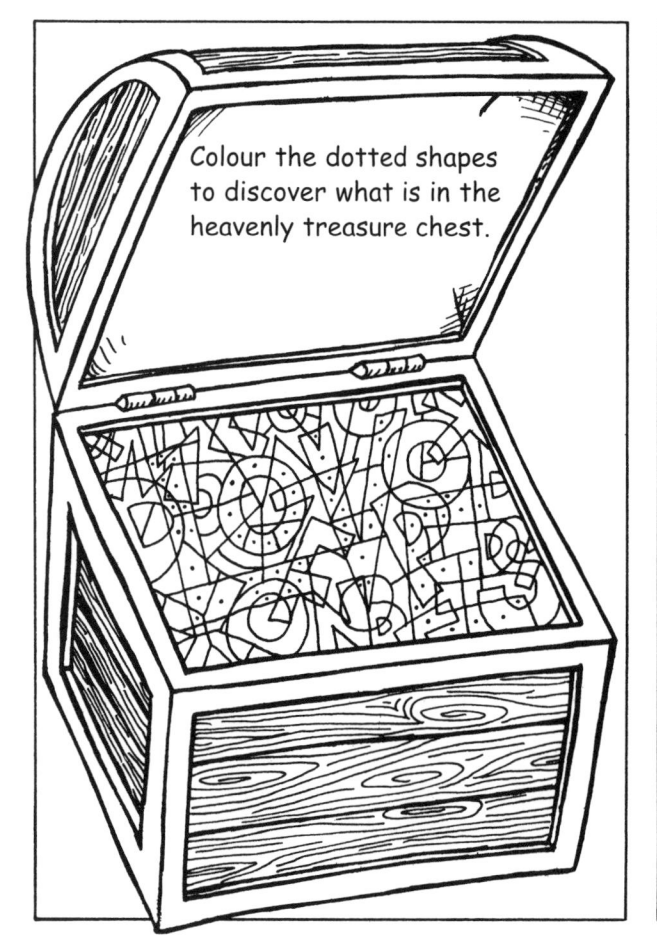

| A | D | E | I | L | N | O | S | U | V | Y |

WORDSEARCH

Find the following words in the grid: COMPLACENT, TRAVEL, GOOD, GETTING, HEAVEN, CAMEL, POSSESSIONS, GIVING, TREASURE, LOVE, NEEDLE, LIGHT, BURDENS, EYE.

Colour the dotted shapes to discover what is in the heavenly treasure chest.

```
C O M P L A C E N T L P
A N E E D L T T I N O G
M E A V E T R E A S V O
E X E L D E E N S K E O
L O B U R D A E N Y L G
R S U L O V S U E Y T N
U S R O L S U G O O F I
S E D V I T R E A V E T
A S E O G H E A V E N T
E S N O H G I V I N G E
R S S G S I V O N G D G
T R A V E L Z D O O G Y
```

54

Week 3: New attitudes – a woman in the synagogue

Thinking about it

What's the point?

This was much more than a physical healing. Jesus doesn't tell the woman, 'You are healed', but 'You are *freed*'! And later, when challenged – ostensibly for healing on the Sabbath – he exposes the true objection by highlighting the point that they are treating the woman less well than an animal, and then by dramatically calling her a 'daughter of Abraham' – a title almost never accorded to women in that patriarchal society. This was a new attitude, and a huge challenge. Could this woman truly 'hold her head up' in the House of God? Some people might see a direct parallel here with the way children are regarded in some (fortunately not all) Churches – probably not in yours, since you are open to using this material!

Doing it

Prayer

Thank you, God,
for this time and place you have given us,
where we can be together as your children –
whatever age we are –
and know that we all belong here because you love us.
Help us to enjoy the things we do
and to learn a little more of how much you love us
and all people. Amen.

From the known to the unknown

Have the children ever tried to make themselves small because they were embarrassed in some way? Can they remember 'keeping their head down' and hoping no one would notice? It's highly probable that this woman's 'spirit that crippled her' was a psychological one of that nature. If so, that makes the healing miracle all the more wonderful.

Tell the story: Luke 13:10-17

(See page 58 for a dramatised version of this story.)

Stand Up and Praise God!

Becky just loved going to worship – but she wished she could take part like everyone else. She really wanted to stand up straight and join in praising God – but somehow she just couldn't. She stooped all the time, and looked at the floor and hoped no one would really notice her. But one day, someone did.

The first Becky knew was when she saw a pair of feet – very ordinary feet, newly washed to come to the synagogue, but obviously belonging to someone who walked a lot. And equally obviously belonging to a man. She hoped he'd move aside and let her go past, but he didn't, he just stood there. Should she ask him to move? Perhaps a polite 'Excuse me' would do the trick. Just as she was wondering, she heard a voice – and at a guess it belonged to the person who also owned the feet. 'Why are you bent over like that?'

Becky wasn't going to say so, but she thought that was a silly question. Still, the voice was kind, and the question obviously well meant. 'I haven't stood up straight for eighteen years,' she answered. 'You don't think I *choose* to be like this, do you?'

'Well,' the man replied, 'you're free from all that, now. From now on, always hold your head up in this place. You belong here – and God wants you here.'

And saying that, he took hold of her hand. What was going on? She felt him lifting her hand, very gently but quite firmly, as if he was trying to help her straighten up. What did he think he was doing!

Becky made an effort, and craned her neck upwards to see who it was. Oh, of course – it was Jesus! She'd seen him around a few times, heard some stories about people he'd healed who were ill – and about some people he'd upset, as well. Gradually, as she looked at him, her back straightened and for the first time in years, she stood up to her full height. It felt a lot better than she'd ever expected it would. All that time when she'd been longing to be able to stand up straight, she'd never realised it could be as good as this. Well, for a start, faces are nicer than feet to look at – usually, anyway – and she could see the beautiful decorations in the building, and get a better idea of what was going on. But the main thing was, she felt part of it – as though she really belonged there. Well, she started shouting for joy. 'Thank God!' she laughed, happily. 'It's wonderful – he's helped me stand up straight again. Hey, look everybody – look at me!'

They were – looking at her, that is. And some of them didn't like it at all.

'Hey! What d'you think you're doing?' The angry voice belonged to old Enoch, the leader of the synagogue. 'You can't do that in my synagogue!' he shouted at Jesus.

'Interesting,' Jesus replied. 'I actually thought the synagogue was God's, not yours.'

'Don't get clever with me,' Enoch thundered. 'You know what I mean. This is the Sabbath – the official day of rest – and no one's allowed to work. We all know you're a healer, so it's work you're doing.' Then he turned to the congregation. 'You've got six days every week to get cured,' he said. 'I don't want to see any of you coming to get healed on the Sabbath. Understood?'

'Oh, get real!' Jesus answered. 'Haven't you ever untied your donkey on the Sabbath and taken it to find water? Well, that's just an animal. This is a woman – a descendant of Abraham, just like you. And don't you think *she* also ought to be untied and set free on the Sabbath?'

Enoch was embarrassed by that – especially when someone from the congregation called out, 'You can't treat a woman as less than an animal!'

'Sexist!' shouted another person.

'Misogynist!' roared another – and Enoch was *really* cross about that. He'd have been even crosser if he'd known what it meant, because he *didn't* actually hate women. He loved his wife very much – but then, she knew her place, of course.

Suddenly, the whole congregation was praising God who had healed Becky.

'Hallelujah!' someone shouted.

'Praise the Lord!' said someone else.

'Amen to that!' responded a few more.

'You can't say that,' shouted Enoch. '*I'm* in charge, and *I'll* say when God is to be praised!'

Poor, sad Enoch! But Becky was happier than she had ever been in her life before!

Respond to the story

Discussion

Why did old Enoch complain about Jesus?
- Because he worked on the Day of Rest?
- Do the children think that was the real reason?

What did Jesus mean by calling the woman 'a descendant of Abraham'?
- That she was as important as everyone else?

How might she have felt, hearing that said about her?

Song

One or more of the following songs might be used here and/or in the all-age worship:

I will enter his gates
I'm gonna clap my hands
Let us sing and praise God
Stand up, walk tall
Zip bam boo

Art and craft

✔ Using A4 card, make large 'labels' to hang on people. (See 'Word and action' in the all-age worship for how this would be used.) Write on them some of the traditional categories by which people are stereotyped. You will certainly need 'Man', 'Woman', 'Young' 'Old', and after that you can tailor them to your local situation. Just one warning – make sure you've got people in the congregation who will enter into the spirit of this and not mind wearing the labels. Alternatively, get the children to come in fancy dress to the all-age worship, and put the labels on them!

Draw or paint a picture of the woman, stooping, among some very tall men!

This is the key picture, but you might want to do others in addition to it, such as:
- Jesus, lifting her up
- Simon pointing and shouting at Jesus
- The crowd cheering and celebrating

Drama: Stand Up and Praise God!

Narrator	Becky just loved going to worship. But it could have been better.
Becky	I'd really love to stand up straight and join in praising God – but somehow I just can't. So I spend the service looking at the floor and hoping no one will really notice me.
Narrator	But one day, someone did. The first Becky knew was when she saw a pair of feet – obviously belonging to someone who walked a lot. And obviously belonging to a man.
Becky	Perhaps he'll move aside and let me go past. No, he's just going to stand there. Should I ask him to move – politely, of course?
Narrator	Just as she was wondering, she heard a voice.
Jesus	Why are you bent over like that?
Becky	I haven't stood up straight for eighteen years. You don't think I *choose* to be like this, do you?
Jesus	Well, you're free from all that, now. From now on, always hold your head up. You belong here – and God wants you here.
Narrator	And saying that, he took hold of her hand, as if he was trying to help her straighten up. What did he think he was doing! Becky made an effort, and craned her neck upwards to see who it was.
Becky	[*Aside*] Oh, of course – Jesus! I've seen him around a few times, heard some stories about people he's healed who were ill – and about some people he's upset, as well.
Narrator	Gradually, as she looked at him, Becky's back straightened and for the first time in years, she stood up to her full height.
Becky	Hey, it feels a lot better than I ever expected it would. All that time I've been longing to be able to stand up straight – I never realised it could be as good as this. Well, for a start, faces are nicer than feet to look at – usually, anyway.
Narrator	But the main thing was, she felt part of it – as though she really belonged there. Well, she started shouting for joy.
Becky	Thank God! It's wonderful – he's helped me stand up straight again. Hey, look everybody – look at me!
Narrator	They *were* – looking at her, that is. And some of them didn't like it at all – especially old Enoch, the leader of the synagogue.
Enoch	Hey! Jesus! What d'you think you're doing? You can't do that in my synagogue!
Jesus	Interesting – I thought the synagogue was God's, not yours.
Enoch	Don't get clever with me – you know what I mean. This is the official day of rest, and no one's allowed to work. We all know you're a healer, so it's work you're doing. [*To congregation*] You've got six days every week to get cured. I don't want to see any of you coming to get healed on the Sabbath. Understood?

Jesus	Oh, get real! Haven't you ever untied your donkey on the Sabbath and taken it to find water? Well, that's just an animal. This is a woman – a descendant of Abraham, just like you. And don't you think she also ought to be untied and set free on the Sabbath?
Narrator	Enoch was embarrassed by that – especially when people from the congregation started calling out –
Worshipper 1	You can't treat a woman as less than an animal!
Worshipper 2	Sexist!
Worshipper 3	Misogynist!
Enoch	That's not true. I do *not* hate women. I love my wife very much – but then, she knows her place, of course – don't you, Ermintrude?
Ermintrude	Yes, dear.
Narrator	Suddenly, the whole congregation was praising God who had healed Becky.
Worshipper 1	Hallelujah!
Worshipper 2	Praise the Lord!
Worshippers	Amen to that!
Enoch	You can't say that. *I'm* in charge, and *I'll* say when God is to be praised!
Narrator	Poor, sad Enoch! But Becky was happier than she had ever been in her life before!

THREE + ONE: A BOOK OF BEGINNINGS

... to set the oppressed free. (Luke 4:18)

The following sentence is a little bit wrong. Can you correct it by changing the words in capitals for others that rhyme with them?

Jesus came to give us STRIFE in all its DULLNESS and to bring good VIEWS to the SHORE.

```
D E S C E N D A N G S k
O S T A N D T A L L A D
F R E P R A I S E G B E
R D A T F R E E C O B S
E E F P S T A N E D I C
M I S O G Y N I S T A E
O T A W O R S H I D T N
M N B E O U N T I E H D
A U B R X M A H A R B A
N B A C D N A B B A T N
S A T A B D H N A T S T
G O H A W O R S H I P G
```

WORDSEARCH
Find the following words in the grid:
STAND TALL, WORSHIP, PRAISE, MISOGYNIST, MAN, GOD, DESCENDANT, SABBATH, SET FREE, UNTIED, ABRAHAM, POWER.

60

Week 4: All-age worship

Opening song

A song praising and celebrating the faithfulness of God

Welcome and statement of the theme

Get one or more of the children to point out or hold up the pictures as you sum up the story:

In Junior Church during the past few weeks, we've been learning about how God offered the world a new beginning in Jesus. We looked at three stories as examples. Firstly, we learned about the man born blind, who received new vision in more ways than one, and came to see God very differently from the way he was portrayed by the religious authorities. Then we looked at the new priorities Jesus represented, especially when talking to the rich young ruler who thought he could earn his way to heaven. And finally we saw how Jesus presented radical new attitudes to the synagogue when he confronted the woman who was bent double and enabled her to stand up straight, hold her head up and act as if she belonged in God's house.

Those three stories are examples of the general picture, but today we're going to concentrate on: [*Name the episode of your choice*]

Prayer

– use whichever is appropriate

Based on Week 1

Loving God,
thank you for the vision you put in front of us
as your people.
We pray that as we worship you,
you will open our eyes to recognise you and your challenge.
Please forgive us for the times we refuse to see
because we're afraid of that challenge,
and help us to go from here filled with a sense of your love
and longing to be caught up in your work. Amen.

Based on Week 2

Loving God,
you call us here together as people of faith.
Help us to respond in faith –
to hear your challenge and not to be afraid
to take the risks of faith that you call us to take.
Please forgive us when our intentions are good
but our faith is too small,
and help us to grow in trust toward you,
so that we may fully enter into your kingdom of love and peace. Amen.

Based on Week 3

Loving God,
we come to celebrate your love
which recognises no differences between us
but loves us all.
We cannot fully understand a love like that,
but we come to celebrate that mystery.
Please forgive us
when we make your love seem small by our prejudices,
and help us to love as you love. Amen.

Word and action

– use whichever is appropriate

From Week 1

Invite the congregation to play a game – it's fun, but it makes a serious point. Put up the donkey picture, and invite some people to have a go at pinning the tail on the donkey. Blindfold each volunteer before they get too close (you don't want them seeing your secret!) and guide them forward to stand in front of the donkey. Then give them the tail and the pin, and let them have a go. Some may notice that they can feel the outline – others may not. If nobody notices, you can secretly whisper to one or two of them what the secret is, and then they should be able to get reasonably close.

Finally, reveal the trick to the congregation. You'll probably get a few groans and calls of 'cheat!' but you can point out that what was not obvious to the congregation, who thought they could see, was much more obvious to the 'blind' people, who got close enough to use another of their senses. *But they had to get close to do it, and be open to other senses than sight.* Now they're going to hear a story about a man who was blind, but who was able to 'see' much more than the sighted people around him.

Now, read the story, either in narrative or dramatised form.

From Week 2

Have the story read, either in narrative or dramatised form.

Divide the congregation into groups, giving each a supply of the card coins, and say that their task is to identify the kind of treasure this church could store up in heaven, by doing practical things for the poorest people – both locally and internationally. Local initiatives might, for example, include a luncheon club, or a visiting scheme for the housebound, individuals buying *The Big Issue* when they see people selling it. From a more world-wide viewpoint, does the church use only fairly traded tea, coffee, etc., and take part in Christian Aid Week? What about a fair-trade stall at church events? Could the church appoint a disaster relief convenor with authority to organise collections, etc? Those are a few examples in case people need help. Ask them to write the ideas they think of on their coins.

After an appropriate time, call the groups to order and ask each group in turn for one item they have written on their coins. (Doing it in turn gives more people a chance, before they find all their ideas have been mentioned already.) Then ask people from each group to bring their coins forward and place them in the treasure chest (or you could pass it round), assuring them that the ideas will be passed to the appropriate meetings, etc., for consideration – so out of this worship should come some practical outreach. Finish by offering the treasure to God in prayer.

From Week 3

Before the service, have a number of seats placed in parts of the church separate from the usual congregational seats. Explain before you begin the activity that the purpose of it is to show how silly it is to pigeonhole people – so no one should be offended by the first part of the activity! Get either the dressed-up children or some volunteers to come forward and explain that you're starting a new approach to worship and Church life, tailored to the individual. And to make it easy to remember who's who you're going to pin some handy labels on people. So who have you got? An 'old' person. Well, of course, they won't want anything new to happen, will they? So you've got a special seat for them where they can sit inconspicuously and not take part. A woman? Well, no offence but we don't want a lot of silly gossip during worship, so we've got a special place for her where she won't disturb people. A 'child'. Now, we have to make very special provision for children, don't we? We don't want the service disrupted by bad behaviour, so for the time being why not go 'over there', and once we've seen that he or she can behave we'll think about a seat in the main part of the church. Now, a 'teenager'. Well, you won't like the kind of music we have here – you're only into all that ultra-modern stuff, and you wouldn't like anything we do. So if you go over to that seat there, we'll get some earphones for you and you can just do your own thing. OK?

When you've finished, get the congregation into groups and ask them to discuss what you've done. You want them to persuade you to let the people back into worship – partly on the basis of human values, but also with some good Christian reasons as well! After a few minutes, call them to order and let the fireworks begin! As each of the volunteers returns to the congregation (if the congregation can't persuade you to do that, you've got *real* problems!!) let them be welcomed with enthusiastic applause. Does all that sound silly? Well, listen to this . . .

Have the story read, either in narrative or dramatised form.

Song 2

Offering

This may be introduced as symbolising our willingness to make our contribution to the new beginning God is longing to make in our lives and communities.

Offertory prayer

> Loving God,
> we thank you for always putting fresh challenges
> before your people,
> and new hope in the world.
> Use these gifts of ourselves and our possessions
> to enable a new beginning in faith
> for us and for others. Amen.

Song 3

Reading

> Isaiah 43:18-21 read from a standard Bible. Introduce it with words such as: through the prophet Isaiah, God calls us to be on the alert, looking for the new things he's doing – the new opportunities he's putting before the Churches and the world today.

Talk (optional)

> If you feel it appropriate (and if time permits) you can point out that Jesus' new beginning challenged the old, accepted religious ideas and practices. That didn't mean he didn't value his traditions, but he never allowed the 'We've always done it this way' mindset to get in the way of his healing and saving work.

Notices and family news

Prayers of intercession

> These could be led entirely by the minister or other adult(s), and/or could include some prayers written by the children themselves – or simply some points that they have raised in discussion.

Song 4

Closing prayer/benediction

Unit 3
Acts – in the Church's beginning, God . . .

Overview of the unit

Theme: God breaks the old barriers

We take three key events:

Week 1: The gift of the Holy Spirit

God sends the Holy Spirit who inspires the disciples to go and spread the Gospel, which they are able to communicate because the gift of tongues breaks down the barriers of language so that the word can spread to all nations.

Week 2: The conversion of Saul

The barriers of prejudice are broken as the Church's fiercest persecutor is dramatically converted and becomes its greatest advocate.

Week 3: The baptism of Cornelius

God breaks through Peter's prejudice and calls him to baptise a non-Jew into the Christian Church. There truly is no limit to God's love!

All-age worship

Here, you may choose to focus on any one of the three subthemes, but place it in the context of the overall story and theme: God's new beginning for the Church. So while the specific theme chosen will be emphasised in the choice of 'Word and action' material, some of the art and craft work the children have done in the other weeks will be used to decorate the church and set the context of the wider story.

Important note

✔ The ticked activities in Weeks 1–3 are intended as the link material for the 'Word and action' slot in the all-age worship. You will only need to do this in one of the three weeks – depending on which week's subtheme is going to be the main emphasis in the service.

Week 1: The gift of the Holy Spirit

Thinking about it

What's the point?

The Holy Spirit, at Pentecost, empowered the disciples with the resources they needed for their time and place. Like Moses, they were given the ability to go and communicate God's word. The barriers of language were broken down and the Gospel began to be heard.

Doing it

Prayer

Loving God,
thank you for bringing us together,
all different people,
and helping us to learn from and understand one another.
Help us to enjoy the time we have here,
and go from here full of your love and your joy. Amen.

From the known to the unknown

Do the children sometimes feel they speak a different language from their parents? Sometimes it can be very difficult to make ourselves understood, even if we speak what is regarded as the same language, because we use words differently. More on that later, but for now here's a story.

Tell the story: Acts 2:1-12

(See page 70 for a dramatised version of this story.)

God Breaks the Language Barrier

The friends of Jesus had a wonderful story to tell. For a time, they'd thought it was all over – the people who hated Jesus had had him killed, but what do you think had happened after that?* God raised him from the dead and gave him new life – and he'd been seen by all his close friends before he went back to heaven. But they had a promise that he'd always be with them, and he'd told them to tell the whole world the Good News that he was alive.

'So what are we waiting for?' Peter was grumbling. 'We've got to do as Jesus said – tell the world. And instead we're all sitting here together, just praying!'

Peter always was the one who went at everything like a bull at a gate – head down, mouth in gear, brain in neutral! 'Jesus also told us,' Andrew reminded him, 'to wait until we get the power we need. I don't know what he meant, but I'm sure we'll know when we get it.'

'But we're missing the boat,' Peter objected. 'This is the great festival – there are people from all over the world here, and we've got to tell them so they can go home and tell their friends.'

* Well, what *do* they think happened?

'Fine,' Thomas chipped in. 'And just how are you going to talk to foreign visitors when none of us can speak any of their languages?'

Peter had to admit, Thomas had a point – but before he could answer, something really strange started happening. It was a sound like a gale blowing through the room – but the air was completely still. The sound got louder and louder – everyone was waiting for the roof to come off the house, but still they didn't feel anything.

Philip, another of the friends, knew something important was going on. 'Didn't Jesus say that God's Spirit was like the wind?' he said. 'Didn't he say something about it blowing and you never knew where it came from or where it went?'

'Oh, heaven save us, he's getting all intellectual!' Peter knew all about nets and fish, but he would never have called himself a deep thinker.

'He's right, though,' Nathanael chipped in. 'That's exactly what Jesus said, and it's *exactly* what's happening now.'

'Never mind all the fancy theories,' Peter snapped. 'We've got to get out there and *do* something. On second thoughts,' his voice took on a panicky note, 'just get out – the room's on fire!'

'You know,' said Philip, calmly, 'I do believe he's right – the room *is* on fire. You know, this is very interesting.'

'Never mind interesting – let's get out!'

'But it's not burning, is it?' Philip mused. 'The room's full of fire, but nothing's getting burnt.'

He was right. Gradually the panic subsided, but Peter was still agitated. 'What's going on?' he said. 'I can't remember anything like this before.'

'Yes, you can,' Philip corrected him. 'Moses – the burning bush – it was on fire but it never got burnt. Don't you see?'

Peter didn't see. But Nathanael did.

'This is the power Jesus promised us!' he exclaimed. 'Just like Moses – God's giving us the power we need to go and do his work. Oh, I say – where's everybody gone?'

When Nathanael got outside he saw the most amazing scene. There was Peter, rattling on nineteen to the dozen – well, there was nothing strange in that. But he was talking Arabic – telling someone from Libya all about Jesus. Then he heard Andrew's voice – but Andrew was speaking in Latin, and he'd never been any good at that – and yet he'd buttonholed a Roman merchant who just couldn't wait to hear more about Jesus.

Just as he was trying to take all this in, a woman came up to him and said, 'What's this all about?'

'I'm really very sorry,' Nathanael answered without stopping to think, 'but I don't speak Turkish. You'll have to ask someone else.'

The woman looked bemused. 'I don't understand,' she said.

'Well, it's really simple enough,' Nathanael said, a little crossly. 'I don't speak your language – go and ask someone who does.'

The woman smiled. 'But if you don't speak my language, how come I'm understanding every word you're saying?'

She was right! Everyone was amazed. The Good News about Jesus was being spread to all the foreign visitors *in their own languages*. 'Well!' said Nathanael. 'So this is what God's Holy Spirit can do. Impressive. *Very* impressive!'

Respond to the story

Discussion

How do the children think the disciples felt when they realised what a gift God had given them?

- Excited?
- Surprised?
- Maybe a little nervous?
- Maybe *very* nervous?

Why did Jesus' friends need the special gift of the Holy Spirit?

- To give them confidence?
- To reassure them of God's power?
- To enable them to do new things?

Why do we still need the gift of the Holy Spirit?

- To give us confidence?
- To help us to tell God's story to others?

Song

One or more of the following songs might be used here and/or in the all-age worship:

God is here, God is present

Hang on, stand still, stay put, hold tight

I'm so excited

Jesus, send me the helper

You've got to move when the Spirit says move

Art and craft

✔ You're going to make some 'flash cards'. (See 'Word and action' in the all-age worship for how these would be used.) Go back to the opening question about children finding it difficult to make parents understand. Can they give any examples of words or phrases that their parents either don't understand, or understand differently? Examples might be computer terminology, or simply words that have become applied as slang – at the time of writing, 'wicked' might mean something radically different in the playground culture from in the Church! Divide a sheet of paper into eight equal sections by folding it, and then write in large letters in each section one of the words or phrases. On a second sheet of paper, write the meanings in a similar fashion. Then, before the next service, photocopy the pages onto different colours of card – one colour for the buzzwords and another for the interpretations. You will need enough cards for each worshipper to be given one, of whichever colour comes to hand, as they enter the church.

Draw or paint a picture of the disciples with tongues of fire over their heads.

This is the key picture, but you might want to do others in addition to it, such as:

- Disciples in the street talking to various different people.

Drama: God Breaks the Language Barrier

Narrator	The friends of Jesus had a wonderful story to tell. For a time, they'd thought it was all over – the people who hated Jesus had had him killed, but God raised him from the dead and gave him new life – and he'd been seen by all his close friends before he went back to heaven. But they had a promise that he'd always be with them, and he'd told them to tell the whole world the Good News that he was alive – and Peter was getting impatient.
Peter	So what are we waiting for? We've got to do as he said – tell the world. And instead we're all sitting here together, just praying!
Narrator	Peter always was the one who went at everything like a bull at a gate – head down, mouth in gear, brain in neutral!
Andrew	Jesus also told us to wait until we get the power we need. I don't know what he meant, but I'm sure we'll know when we get it.
Peter	But, Andrew, this is the great festival – there are people from all over the world here, and we've got to tell them so they can go home and tell their friends. That's right, isn't it, Thomas?
Thomas	Fine – and just how are you going to talk to foreign visitors when none of us can speak any of their languages?
Narrator	Peter had to admit, Thomas had a point – but before he could answer, something really strange started happening. It sounded like a gale blowing through the room – but the air was completely still. It got louder and louder, but still they didn't feel anything. Philip, another of the friends, knew something important was going on.
Philip	Didn't Jesus say that God's Spirit was like the wind? Didn't he say something about it blowing and you never knew where it came from or where it went?
Peter	Oh, heaven save us, he's getting all intellectual!
Narrator	Peter knew all about nets and fish, but he would never have called himself a deep thinker.
Nathanael	He's right, though – that's exactly what Jesus said, and it's *exactly* what's happening now.
Peter	Never mind the theories, Nathanael. We've got to get out and *do* something. On second thoughts, just get out – the room's on fire!
Philip	[*Calmly*] You know, I do believe he's right – the room *is* on fire. This is very interesting.
Peter	Never mind interesting – let's get out!
Philip	But it's not burning, is it? Lots of fire, but nothing's burning.
Narrator	He was right. Gradually the panic subsided, but Peter was still agitated.
Peter	What's going on? I can't remember anything like this before.

Philip	Yes you can. Moses – the burning bush – it was on fire but it never got burnt. Don't you see?
Narrator	Peter didn't see. But Nathanael did.
Nathanael	This is the Holy Spirit Jesus promised us! Just like Moses – God's giving us the power we need to go and do his work. Oh, I say – where's everybody gone?
Narrator	When Nathanael got outside he was amazed. Peter was rattling on nineteen to the dozen – nothing strange in that, but he was telling someone from Libya about Jesus – in Arabic. Then he heard Andrew speaking Latin – he'd buttonholed a Roman merchant who just couldn't wait to hear more about Jesus. Just then, a woman came up to Nathanael.
Woman	What's this all about?
Nathanael	I'm really very sorry, but I don't speak Turkish. You'll have to ask someone else.
Woman	I don't understand.
Nathanael	Well, it's really simple enough: I don't speak your language – go and ask someone who does.
Woman	But if you don't speak my language, how come I'm understanding every word you're saying?
Narrator	She was right! Everyone was amazed. The Good News about Jesus was being spread to all the foreign visitors *in their own languages*.
Nathanael	So this is God's Holy Spirit at work. Impressive. *Very* impressive!

THREE + ONE: A BOOK OF BEGINNINGS

The Holy Spirit gives life. Colour the flames to bring this picture to life!

I will pour out my Spirit. (Joel 2:28)

The Holy Spirit helps us to understand things more clearly. So use the key below to colour this picture and discover a message.

1 = Blue 3 = Red 5 = Green
2 = Brown 4 = Pink 6 = Light Brown or Yellow

WORDSEARCH

Find the following words in the grid below: COMMUNICATE, WAITING, FIRE, WIND, NEW LIFE, SPIRIT, POWER, PROMISE, GOOD NEWS, JESUS, BROKEN BARRIERS.

```
G O O D N E D S P I R C
N M B A R R I E R S O O
I M R O M I S E P U K M
T U O M M U N I C S E M
I N K G O O R N E E N U
A I E W I I N D O J E N
W I N D T X G O O D N I
N C W E P R O M I D E C
E W S N W L I F E N W A
E R B A R R I E D E S T
W I L N D P R O M I S E
L I F F E F I R E W O P
```

72

Week 2: The conversion of Saul

Thinking about it

What's the point?

Saul was a member of the religious group that had hated Jesus the most – and it showed! He often said later that if there was one person who didn't deserve to have God care about him, it was himself! So this story is all about what *God* can do, because he loves us – whether we actually deserve that love or not.

Doing it

Prayer

Thank you, Lord,
for loving us so much,
even when we don't deserve it.
Help us to care for one another as much as that,
and to show your love to other people.
Please be with us in all we do this morning,
and help us to learn about your power and love.
Amen.

From the known to the unknown

Have the children ever known that they were being unfair to someone they didn't like – but carried on just the same? (A little self-disclosure on the part of the teacher might encourage them here – we've all done it at some time or other!) The Good News is that God can help us when we're being like that – if he could help the person in this story, he can help anybody!

Tell the story: Acts 9:1-20

(See page 76 for a dramatised version of this story.)

From Killer to Christian

This story is about Saul. Saul was a Pharisee – a kind of religious lawyer – and like almost all the Pharisees, he hated Jesus. But now that Jesus was dead, Saul couldn't really hate him properly any more, so he started hating Jesus' friends. Oh, sorry – did I say that Jesus was dead? Silly – I meant, of course, that Saul *thought* Jesus was dead. The religious leaders had done a very thorough job of making sure he was, but he'd hardly been buried a couple of days when his friends were telling everybody he'd risen from the dead and was alive. Of course, Saul and the other Pharisees tried to say they were making it all up, but people still believed it. After all, why were Jesus' friends so happy if it wasn't true? So Saul hated Jesus' friends and wanted to get rid of them all. One of them, Stephen, had already been killed. Saul had seen him die, and it had made him hate the Christians all the more, because he just wouldn't stop praising God and saying Jesus was alive, even while they were torturing him to death. And Saul just hated people like that.

So Saul went to see the chief priests. 'Just say the word,' he said, 'and I'll hunt Jesus' friends down, and see they all get what's coming to them. We've got to kill them all, before any more people start believing in him. I'm going to start at Damascus, because I know there are some of them there.'

'Sounds good to me,' said the High Priest. 'We don't want people saying Jesus is alive after we had him killed, now do we? I mean, does that make us look silly, or does that make us look silly?'

So Saul got his warrant from the High Priest, and set off for Damascus with some soldiers of the High Priest's bodyguard to help him. Some of the soldiers couldn't really see what all the fuss was about.

'Why are you so worked up about these people, Saul?' asked Marcus.

'Because they're horrible liars,' Saul ranted, 'and they don't love and respect God like I do – that's why I'm going to kill them all, slowly and horribly, to show that I love God more than they do.'

'I see,' answered Marcus, thoughtfully. 'You're sure there isn't a deeper psychological reason for all this?'*

Now, Saul was a well-educated man, but he'd never heard that word before. 'Psycho-what-al?' he asked.

'Oh, you won't have heard of it,' answered Marcus, 'but give it a couple of thousand years and psychology will be all the rage. What you're doing is a classic case.'

Saul wanted to tell Marcus to mind his own business, but he couldn't help being curious. 'It is?'

'That's right – one day everyone will know about it. Deep down, you're not as sure of yourself as you like to think, and killing Christians is your way of – '

'Mind your own business,' Saul snapped. 'Shut up, or it will be worse for you.'

Marcus shut up, but Saul couldn't help noticing the little knowing smile that hovered around his face.

What happened next wiped the smile away, though – and it was something even Marcus couldn't explain with his fancy new science. Saul saw the light – literally. A blinding light – again, literally. One second he was thinking how nice it would be to add Marcus to the hit list, and the next he was on the ground, shaking like a broken washing machine and as blind as a one-eyed needle. None of the soldiers could see the light – God had aimed it just at Saul, and God's a good shot – so they were a bit gobsmacked at first. But they heard the voice. *Everyone* heard the voice.

'Saul, Saul – why are you being so horrible to me?'

Saul was by now a gibbering wreck. 'Who are you? Please tell me who you are.'

---

* An inference drawn from Acts 26:14.

'I'm Jesus – the one you're being so rotten to. You hurt my friends, you hurt me. OK? And why are you fighting against your own conscience? Even a cow knows better than to kick when it's prodded.'*

Marcus didn't say 'I told you so' – he was much too frightened to be a smart Alec.

'Anyway,' Jesus went on, 'stop grovelling in that undignified fashion, and go to Damascus. You'll find one of my friends there who can help you.'

So that's what Saul did. He went to Damascus, met Ananias, changed his name to Paul, and from that time on he couldn't stop telling people that Jesus was alive. Now how could anyone change that much, that quickly? God knows!

Respond to the story

Discussion

How do the children think Saul felt when he was fighting against Jesus?
- Angry?
- Unhappy?

How do they think he felt when he finally faced up to things and changed?
- Relieved?
- Longing to tell people about it?

Song

One or more of the following songs might be used here and/or in the all-age worship:

God is here, God is present
Lord, the light of your love
Majesty
Oh! Oh! Oh! How good is the Lord
We're going to shine like the sun

Art and craft

✔ On a large piece of paper, draw a triangle of light, as though a light is shining down from the top of the page. (See 'Word and action' in the all-age worship for how this would be used.) Darken the areas either side, either with paint or black paper, and write a heading over the top, such as '[Name of your church] sees the light'.

Draw or paint a picture of Saul on the ground with a 'spotlight' from above shining on him.

This is the key picture, but you might want to do others in addition to it, such as:
- Saul talking to the High Priest
- Saul and the soldiers on the road

* Acts 26:14

Drama: From Killer to Christian

Narrator: This story is about Saul. Saul was a Pharisee – a kind of religious lawyer – and like almost all the Pharisees, he hated Jesus. But now that Jesus was dead Saul couldn't really hate him properly any more, so he started hating Jesus' friends. Oh, sorry – did I say that Jesus was dead? I meant that Saul *thought* Jesus was dead. The religious leaders had made sure he was, but he'd hardly been buried a couple of days when his friends were telling everybody he'd risen from the dead and was alive. Of course, Saul and the other Pharisees tried to say they were making it all up, but why were Jesus' friends so happy if it wasn't true? So Saul hated Jesus' friends and wanted to get rid of them all. One of them, Stephen, had already been killed. Saul had seen him die, and it had made him hate the Christians all the more, because Stephen just wouldn't stop praising God and saying Jesus was alive, even while they were torturing him to death. And Saul just hated people like that. So Saul went to see the High Priest.

Saul: Just say the word, and I'll hunt Jesus' friends down, and see they all get what's coming to them. We've got to kill them all, before any more people start believing in him. I'm going to start at Damascus, because I know there are some of them there.

High Priest: Sounds good to me. We don't want people saying Jesus is alive after we had him killed, now do we? I mean, does that make us look silly, or does that make us look silly?

Narrator: So Saul got his warrant from the High Priest, and set off for Damascus with some soldiers of the High Priest's bodyguard to help him. Marcus, one of the soldiers, couldn't really see what all the fuss was about.

Marcus: Why are you so worked up about these people, Saul?

Saul: [*Ranting, madly*] Because they're horrible liars, and they don't love and respect God like I do – so I'm going to kill them all, slowly and horribly, to show that I love God more than they do.

Marcus: [*Thoughtfully*] I see. You're sure there isn't a deeper psychological reason for all this?

Saul: [*Baffled*] Psycho-what-al?

Marcus: Oh, you won't have heard of it, but in a couple of thousand years psychology will be all the rage. What you're doing is a classic case.

Narrator: Saul wanted to tell Marcus to mind his own business, but he couldn't help being curious.

Saul: It is?

Marcus: That's right – one day everyone will know about it. Deep down, you're not as sure of yourself as you like to think, and killing Christians is your way of –

Saul: [*Snaps*] Mind your own business! Shut up, or it'll be worse for you!

Narrator	Marcus shut up, but Saul couldn't help noticing the little knowing smile that hovered around his face. What happened next wiped the smile away, though – and it was something even Marcus couldn't explain with his fancy new science. Saul saw the light – literally. A blinding light – again, literally. One second he was thinking how nice it would be to add Marcus to the hit list, and the next he was on the ground, shaking like a broken washing machine and as blind as a one-eyed needle. None of the soldiers could see the light – God had aimed it just at Saul, and God's a good shot – so they were a bit gobsmacked at first. But they heard the voice. *Everyone* heard the voice.
Jesus	Saul, Saul – why are you being so horrible to me?
Narrator	Saul was by now a gibbering wreck.
Saul	Who are you? Please tell me who you are.
Jesus	I'm Jesus – the one you're being rotten to. You hurt my friends, you hurt me. OK? Why are you fighting your own conscience? Even a cow knows better than to kick when it's prodded.
Narrator	Marcus didn't say 'I told you so' – he was much too frightened to be a smart Alec.
Jesus	Anyway, stop grovelling in that undignified fashion, and go to Damascus. You'll find one of my friends there who can help you.
Narrator	So that's what Saul did. He went to Damascus, met Ananias, changed his name to Paul, and from that time on he couldn't stop telling people that Jesus was alive. Now, how could anyone change that much, that quickly? God knows!

THREE + ONE: A BOOK OF BEGINNINGS

What do you think the soldiers are saying?

A new spirit I will put within you. (Ezekiel 36:26)

WORDSEARCH

Find the following words in the grid: PHARISEE, DAMASCUS, JESUS, SAUL, CONVERSION, ANANIAS, BLINDING, KICKING, ALIVE, LIGHT, ROAD, HIGH PRIEST.

```
P H A R I S E E H I G C
H I A L I G H A N A V O
A G N I D N I L B B I N
R H A G R V L I G S D V
I P S H U N T V C A N E
S P R T P R I E S I I R
D G N I K C I K W N L S
E A F J E S U S V A B I
S A O L A S C U S N L O
A A N R N I T U S A I N
U H U T S U C S A M A D
P N A L I S E E A L I V
```

Saul can't see. Can you guide him to Ananias?

Week 3: Peter and Cornelius

Thinking about it

What's the point?

The Church often has difficulty with people who are different. Many people outside the Church today think (rightly or wrongly) they wouldn't be accepted if they came in. The question is, should we expect people to conform before they can be allowed in?

Doing it

Prayer

Loving God,
thank you for giving us this time to be together,
even though we're all so different.
There aren't two of us that are exactly alike,
but you don't love us less because of it.
Help us today to learn more of your love,
and find better ways of relating to each other. Amen.

From the known to the unknown

Have the children ever felt 'left out'? Perhaps they've been with people who don't share their taste in music, or support their team. Or perhaps some of them simply aren't into those things, and *that's* why they get left out? (If any of them say they feel left out at church, this is a wonderful opportunity to take that seriously and not deny it!)

Well, even the closest friends of Jesus made the mistake of shutting people out sometimes, and they had to be helped to learn better ways – as this story will show.

Tell the story: Acts 10-11

(See page 82 for a dramatised version of this story.)

But They're Different from Us

'Hey, Simon, what time's dinner?' Peter called. You remember Peter – one of Jesus' closest friends? Well, he'd given up catching fish for a living and taken up a different kind of fishing – fishing for people, as Jesus had called it. He went all over the world telling people about Jesus, and especially how he had risen from the dead, and that they could be Jesus' friends too, if they wanted to. That's how he came to be staying with his friend, Simon the leatherworker, at Joppa.

'Oh, it'll be a while yet,' Simon answered. 'Why, are you hungry?'

'Starving!' Peter answered, 'but don't worry, I'll go upstairs and pray for a bit.'

'Pray for a bit of what?' Simon asked. 'Food, or patience?'

'You know what I mean,' Peter smiled. 'I'll be on the flat roof – I take it you've had the safety rail mended?' Peter went up without waiting for an answer and started praying while Simon started getting dinner, muttering to himself as he did so.

'"What time's dinner?" "What time's breakfast?" Does that man think of nothing but food? It wouldn't be so bad if he weren't such a fussy eater. "Can't eat this, it's fattening" – "Don't give me that, it's got salt in it" – "This gives me spots" – "That's against my religion". There's just no pleasing some people.'

Meanwhile, Peter was trying to pray, but he was finding it difficult – kept getting images of 90 per cent fat-free kosher fisherman's pie that made his mouth water and drowned his concentration. Then, as if that wasn't bad enough, God gave him a vision of food. It looked like a big sailcloth coming down from above, held by the four corners. As it got lower Peter looked over the side and saw all kinds of animals.

'Go on, Peter,' God said to him. 'Kill one of those and eat it.'

'Oh, I can't do that,' Peter said. 'It's not proper food – it's unclean.'

'If I say something's clean, don't you go contradicting me!' God answered, sternly – and lowered the sailcloth again. 'Go on, Peter – eat something.'

'No, really, I couldn't – I've never eaten anything like that,' Peter gabbled.

'Don't you listen?' God asked him. 'If I say it's clean, it's clean, so don't argue.'

Down came the sailcloth again – Peter's last chance, but he messed it up again and God took the sailcloth away.

'I wonder what all that was about?' Peter mused. 'Knowing God, there's probably some kind of message in it for me – like Son, like Father.'

Just then, Simon called out, 'Peter – you've got some visitors.' Peter went down to see what they wanted.

'We've come from our boss, Cornelius – he's an officer in the Roman army. God's told him to send for you, and he wants you to come straight away.'

Peter was surprised. 'Me – a good Jew – God wants me to go into the house of a Roman soldier? Go on – I'm not swallowing that! Hang on a minute – "swallowing that"? Oh, right. I get it. So *that* was the message, then.'

So Peter went with the servants to Cornelius' house.

'I'm really glad you've come,' said Cornelius. 'I didn't think you would because I know what you Jews think about going into Romans' houses.'

'Well,' Peter answered, 'let's just say God's taught me that it takes all kinds to make a pasta.'

Cornelius looked puzzled. 'Eh? What's a pasta? Oh, never mind. Look, I want to know about this Jesus fellow – and how I can become one of his followers, too.'

'This is wonderful!' Peter exclaimed. 'So God can save anybody at all. No one's a hopeless case – not even a Roman! Oh, sorry, Cornelius, no offence.'

Peter went on and told Cornelius all about Jesus – the great things he had done, the way he'd been killed by sad, jealous people, and how God had raised him back to life and he's alive now.

UNIT 3: WEEK 3

Suddenly, as he spoke, God's Holy Spirit filled the room and Cornelius said, 'That's it – I want to be baptised. Now!'

In no time at all, Peter had baptised Cornelius and made him officially a friend of Jesus. 'Now,' he said. 'Time to celebrate! What about something to eat – anything you've got will do, I'm not fussy.'

Respond to the story

Discussion

Can the children see the connection between the vision of food and the call to visit Cornelius?

- Peter thought some kinds of foods were not good enough for him
- He also thought some kinds of *people* were not good enough for God

How do the children think he felt about going into a Roman soldier's house for the first time?

- Nervous?
- Curious?
- Needing all his faith in God to do it?
- Excited about the new ground he was breaking?

Song

One or more of the following songs might be used here and/or in the all-age worship:

God forgave my sin
God's love is deeper
I'm black, I'm white, I'm short, I'm tall
Nobody's a nobody
We're going to shine like the sun

Art and craft

✔ Get the children to draw some pictures of different creatures. (See 'Word and action' in the all-age worship for how this would be used.) You could either use a flipchart page and divide it into four, or you could use four separate pieces of A4 or A3 paper. You will need one picture of a mammal (e.g. a horse) one snake, one fish and one insect. The pictures don't need to be brilliantly artistic – on the other hand, they could be imaginative cartoon-style pictures, according to what talents the children have. The important thing is simply that they're recognisable as being from distinct groups. Think about where they will be displayed during the service.

Draw or paint a picture of Peter talking to the centurion, Cornelius.

This is the key picture, but you might want to do others in addition to it, such as:

- The sailcloth full of animals
- Peter on the roof, praying

Drama: But They're Different from Us

Peter   Hey, Simon, what time's dinner?

Narrator   That was Peter. You remember Peter – one of Jesus' closest friends? Well, he'd given up catching fish for a living and taken up fishing for people, as Jesus had called it. He went everywhere telling people about Jesus, and how he had risen from the dead, and that they could be Jesus' friends too. That's how he came to be staying with his friend, Simon the leatherworker, at Joppa.

Simon   Oh, dinner will be a while yet. Why, are you hungry?

Peter   Starving! But don't worry, I'll go upstairs and pray for a bit.

Simon   Pray for a bit of what? Food, or patience?

Peter   You know what I mean. I'll be on the flat roof – I take it you've had the safety rail mended?

Narrator   Peter went up without waiting for an answer and started praying while Simon started getting dinner.

Simon   Does that man think of nothing but food? It wouldn't be so bad if he weren't such a fussy eater. 'Can't eat this, it's fattening' – 'Don't give me that, it's got salt in it' – 'This gives me spots' – 'That's against my religion'. There's just no pleasing some people.

Narrator   Meanwhile, Peter was trying to pray, but he was finding it difficult – kept getting images of 90 per cent fat-free kosher fisherman's pie that made his mouth water and drowned his concentration. Then, as if that wasn't bad enough, God gave him a vision of food. It looked like a big sailcloth coming down from above, held by the four corners. As it got lower Peter looked over the side and saw all kinds of animals. Then God spoke.

God   Go on, Peter, kill one of those and eat it.

Peter   Oh, I can't do that, it's not proper food – it's unclean.

God   If I say something's clean, don't you go contradicting me!

Narrator   God lowered the sailcloth again.

God   Go on, Peter – eat something.

Peter   No, really, I couldn't – I've never eaten anything like that.

God   Don't you listen? If I say it's clean, it's clean, so don't argue.

Narrator   Down came the sailcloth again – Peter's last chance, but he messed it up again and God took the sailcloth away.

Peter   I wonder what all that was about? Knowing God, there's probably some kind of message in it for me – like Son, like Father.

Simon   [*Calls*] Peter – you've got some visitors.

Servant 1   We've come from our boss, Cornelius.

Servant 2	He's an officer in the Roman army.
Servant 3	God's told him to send for you – he wants you to come now.
Peter	[*Surprised*]. Me? God wants me to go into the house of a Roman? No offence, you understand, just that we consider Romans unclean – a technical thing. God can't want me to go there – I'm not swallowing that! Hang on a minute – 'swallowing that'? Oh, right. I get it. So *that* was the point of the vision, then.
Narrator	So Peter went with the servants to meet Cornelius.
Cornelius	I'm really glad you've come. I didn't think you would because I know what you Jews think about going into Romans' houses.
Peter	Well, let's just say God's taught me that it takes all kinds to make a pasta.
Cornelius	[*Puzzled*] Eh? What's a pasta? Oh, never mind. Look, I want to know about Jesus— and how I can become one of his followers, too.
Peter	This is wonderful! So God can save anybody. No one's a hopeless case – not even a Roman! Oh, sorry, Cornelius, no offence.
Narrator	Peter went on and told Cornelius all about Jesus – the great things he had done, the way he'd been killed by sad, jealous people, and how God had raised him back to life and he's alive now. Suddenly, as he spoke, God's Holy Spirit filled the room.
Cornelius	That's it – I want to be baptised. Now!
Narrator	In no time at all, Peter had baptised Cornelius and made him officially a friend of Jesus.
Peter	Now – time to celebrate! What about something to eat – anything you've got will do, I'm not fussy.

THREE + ONE: A BOOK OF BEGINNINGS

How many different animals can you see in the sailcloth?

Help Peter find Cornelius' house.

Starting with E find the message running through the grid.

A	F	T	H	C	N	M	O	D	S	E	R
V	T	H	S	J	O	W	Q	O	U	P	X
A	E	G	H	L	W	T	Y	J	S	B	T
F	V	D	G	B	O	D	W	A	E	F	H
B	E	C	G	O	D	S	E	F	J	H	J
T	R	A	G	H	W	J	O	V	V	Q	K
H	Y	G	N	E	G	D	S	E	A	I	S
U	O	Z	B	Y	K	N	D	G	Z	O	T
L	N	N	O	X	T	E	J	J	T	D	M
O	E	C	A	N	G	I	K	K	T	E	Q
N	A	C	Z	B	N	R	R	L	J	R	Y
P	F	R	L	E	A	F	L	O	X	T	P

84

Week 4: All-age worship

Opening song

A song praising and celebrating the faithfulness of God.

Welcome and statement of the theme

Get one or more of the children to point out or hold up the pictures as you sum up the story:

In Junior Church during the past few weeks, we've been learning about how the Church began, after Jesus had ascended to heaven, and some of the ways God offered a new start to the Church and to the world.

We read about the gift of the Holy Spirit, breaking down the barriers of language so that the Good News of Jesus could be told to everybody, and we saw about the dramatic conversion of Saul who had been a fearsome enemy of Christians until Jesus changed him into one of his greatest missionaries. And finally, we saw how God extended the new beginning to the whole world, when the first non-Jew was accepted into the Church – but God had to do some work on Peter's prejudices first.

That's the general picture, but today we're going to concentrate on: [*Name the episode of your choice*].

Prayer

– use whichever is appropriate

Based on Week 1

Loving God,
we meet here like your friends so long ago,
praying that you will pour out your Spirit on us
and give us the gifts of faith we need
to be your people in the world.
Please forgive us
for the lack of commitment we sometimes feel,
and give us confidence to go from here full of joy
to tell your Good News to the world. Amen.

Based on Week 2

Loving God,
meet us here as you met Saul on the road,
give us a new vision of your greatness,
and inspire us to be your people in the world.
Please forgive us when we fight against your call to change,
and help us to trust more
in the abundance of your grace.
Through Jesus Christ, our Lord. Amen.

Based on Week 3

Loving God,
thank you for being such a great God –
greater than our little minds can hold,
and great enough to break the bounds of our prejudices.
Please forgive us when we judge others as less worthy
because of their background or their lifestyle,
and help us to be open to all in your name.
Amen.

Word and action

– use whichever is appropriate

From Week 1

Get the stewards to give the cards to worshippers as they arrive, and then hand any remaining cards to you as the service begins. Now, check that everyone has a card and ask them to pair them up. They will need to talk to one another, comparing cards, to see whether they can pair up a word with its meaning. If they get really stuck, you have the leftover cards and can help.

Although they will obviously begin by comparing with the people immediately around them, at least some people will need to get up and move to a different place, to consult more widely. After a time, call people to order and go through your own full set of cards. Pin up each word in turn and see whether the congregation can now give you its meaning, at which point you can pin the interpretation alongside the word.

You can then point out that if the Church is to communicate with present-day culture, it is going to have to make this kind of an effort. We can and should pray for the gifts we need, but we also know that the Holy Spirit often works through the company of God's people. So is he calling us to listen more carefully to one another, and especially to those whose language seems different, in an attempt to understand and communicate?

Now, read the story – either as narrative or drama.

From Week 2

Have the story read in either narrative or dramatised form, and then point out that when Saul saw the light he recognised that a complete change of attitude and outlook was required because God was doing something new. Either divide the congregation into groups to discuss, or 'brainstorm' with everyone together, the question of what new situations are arising in your area which the Church needs to respond to, writing them up in the light area of the board as you do so. Is God calling the Church to change and renewal in its mission, its worship or its general lifestyle?

For example, there might be demographic changes: a once firmly residential area now becoming more commercial. Or perhaps your village or suburb has become a 'dormitory' with fewer people around during the day. Do more people have to work on Sundays, making traditional worship patterns difficult? Has a school or other establishment recently closed or opened? Are employment opportunities opening up or closing down in the area? Has some focus of community activity recently been lost or a new one begun? Has the average age of the population changed?

Emphasise to the congregation that you are not looking for instant answers to the questions these changes might pose – you simply want them to be identified. The first stage of responding is to recognise the change. Later will come questions about what that change will involve. For now, you might end up like poor Saul – blinded by the revelation and needing time to reflect. The important thing is that the challenge will have been heard. Trust in God for the grace to respond!

From Week 3

Draw attention to the display of creatures, and either divide the congregation into groups for discussion or simply 'brainstorm' this question with the whole group: which is the odd one out? It could be the fish, because it lives in water, but so do some kinds of snake – and there are flying fish, as well, and flightless birds, and . . .

Clearly it's not really very easy to decide which is the odd one out. They're all quite distinct, and yet they're essentially similar. Especially so in one vitally important respect: they're all part of God's creation.

So you can reflect on how important it is to remember that people are all distinctive – no two the same – and yet have vital things in common, not least that we are all created in the image of God.

Now have the story read, either in narrative or dramatised form.

Song 2

Offering

This may be introduced as a sign of our willingness to offer ourselves to God so that he can equip and use us to offer a new beginning to the world (beginning with ourselves!)

Offertory prayer

Loving God,
you give us so much –
accept what we offer here as a sign of our gratitude,
but also of our faith
as we respond to your invitation
to be your people in the world. Amen.

Song 3

Reading

John 13:34-35 read from a standard Bible. Introduce it with words such as: As he offers us a new beginning, Jesus gives us a new commandment. And he makes it sound so simple!

Talk (optional)

If you feel it appropriate (and if time permits) you can comment that Jesus' new commandment puts all the other stories into perspective. There is no point-scoring here, but just a burning desire that the love of Jesus should be known and enjoyed by all people.

Notices and family news

Prayers of intercession

These could be led entirely by the minister or other adult(s), and/or could include some prayers written by the children themselves – or simply some points that they have raised in discussion.

Song 4

Closing prayer/benediction